ACADEMIC SKILLS PROBLEMS
Fourth Edition Workbook

ACADEMIC SKILLS PROBLEMS

Fourth Edition Workbook

EDWARD S. SHAPIRO

THE GUILFORD PRESS
New York   London

©2011 The Guilford Press
A Division of Guilford Publications, Inc.
72 Spring Street, New York, NY 10012
www.guilford.com

Printed in the United States of America

This book is printed on acid-free paper.

Last digit is print number: 9   8   7   6   5   4   3   2

ISBN 978-1-60918-021-8

About the Author

Edward S. Shapiro, PhD, is Director of the Center for Promoting Research to Practice and Professor in the School Psychology Program at Lehigh University, Bethlehem, Pennsylvania. He is the 2006 winner of the Senior Scientist Award given by the Division of School Psychology of the American Psychological Association in recognition of a senior member of the field who has provided a sustained program of outstanding theoretical and research activity. He is a past Editor of *School Psychology Review,* the official journal of the National Association of School Psychologists. Dr. Shapiro has written numerous books and other publications in the areas of curriculum-based assessment, behavioral assessment, behavioral interventions, and pediatric school psychology. He is best known for his work in curriculum-based assessment and nonstandardized methods of assessing academic skills problems. Among his many projects, Dr. Shapiro has recently completed a federal project focused on the development of a multi-tiered, response-to-intervention (RTI) model in two districts in Pennsylvania. He has been working as a consultant to facilitate the implementation of RTI with the Pennsylvania Department of Education as well as with many individual school districts across the country. He also codirects a training grant from the U.S. Department of Education to train preservice school psychologists as facilitators and developers of RTI implementation.

Contents

STEP 2. ASSESSING INSTRUCTIONAL PLACEMENT

STEP 3. INSTRUCTIONAL MODIFICATION

STEP 4. PROGRESS MONITORING

List of Forms

Introduction

THE PURPOSE OF THIS WORKBOOK is to provide forms, instructions, and other materials to supplement *Academic Skills Problems: Direct Assessment and Intervention* (4th edition). The workbook offers elaboration and detail of material covered in the text and also provides additional forms to supplement those in the text. Some forms in the text are duplicated in the workbook for ease in copying; users of the manual are granted permission from the publisher to copy and modify these forms for their personal use. Although the workbook can certainly be used on its own, its purpose is to complement, rather than stand independent from, the text.

The workbook also offers opportunities for learning, practicing, and mastering many of the skills discussed in the text. For example, a complete manual related to the use of the Behavioral Observation of Students in Schools (BOSS) observation code is provided. In addition, information is included on using the BOSS software (available from Pearson Assessment; *www.pearsonassessments.com/pai*), which is designed to be used as an alternative to the BOSS paper-and-pencil version. Full definitions of the BOSS behavioral categories, as well as instructions for collecting information, scoring the observations, and interpreting the data, are given. Also included are forms for completing teacher and student interviews, along with a useful checklist for obtaining teacher reports for academic behavior.

With the increasing development of response to intervention (RTI) as a method for delivering needed services to all students, especially at the elementary level, resources are provided that support the processes of assessment and data-based decision making. In particular, forms useful for organizing data from universal screening and from progress monitoring and forms that document team decision making related to instructional decisions are all provided.

In the area of conducting the direct assessment of academic skills, the workbook offers additional instructions and practice exercises in the assessment process. In particular, detailed explanations of using such measures as "digits correct per minute" and "correct letter sequences" to score math and spelling, respectively, are provided. The workbook also offers a description of and exercises in how to graph data, collect local norms, and other tasks related to a direct assessment of academic skills.

The workbook follows the model of assessment described in the *Academic Skills Problems* text and depicted in Figure 1. The first section, corresponding to the first step of the assessment process—assessing the academic environment (see Figure 2)—provides materials for interviewing teachers and students, conducting direct observations, and using informant report data (teacher rating scale). The next section, corresponding to Step 2 of the process—assessing instructional placement—provides information related to the processes involved in the direct assessment of academic skills (in particular, details about the assessment of reading, math, spelling, and written language). This section contains information on both the use of short- and long-term data-collection procedures.

The third section of the workbook offers details on the use of two powerful instructional interventions: the "folding-in" technique and "cover–copy–compare." The fourth section, corresponding to Step 4 of the model—progress monitoring—provides important information about the graphic display of data, how to collect local norms, and the process of goal setting. The final section offers materials specifically related to the process of RTI, with particular attention to the data-based decision-making component of RTI.

Throughout, readers will find detailed "how-to" explanations offered in a step-by-step fashion. Practice exercises are also provided, and readers are encouraged to develop their own exercises modeled on those in the workbook.

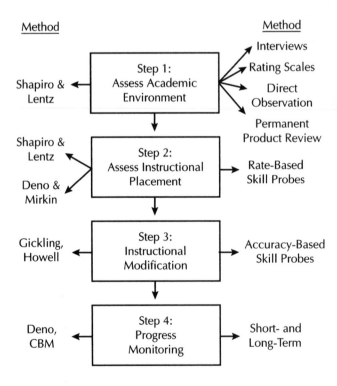

FIGURE 1. Integrated model of CBA. Adapted from Shapiro (1990, p. 334). Copyright 1990 by the National Association of School Psychologists. Adapted by permission of the author.

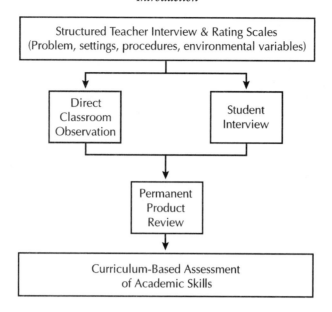

FIGURE 2. Flowchart of procedures for assessing academic skills.

Assessing the Academic Environment

Teacher Interview

THE ASSESSMENT PROCESS BEGINS WITH THE TEACHER INTERVIEW. Several forms are provided to facilitate the interview. The first, which is also printed in the text, suggests the specific questions that should be addressed for each academic area when interviewing teachers. Designed primarily to be completed during a face-to-face meeting with a teacher, the form can also be given to the teacher to fill out before the interview actually occurs. When the form is used in this way, the information provided by the teacher can be used as the context for more in-depth discussion. In the interview process, it is important to learn from the teacher the nature of interventions that have already been tried or are currently in place. In addition, obtaining an understanding of the "big picture" of skill development in reading and mathematics is a critical part of fully understanding the student's problem from the teacher's perspective. In reading, assessing a student's knowledge base in phonemic awareness, alphabetic principle, vocabulary, fluency, and comprehension is essential. In mathematics, information on a student's acquisition of computational skills and concepts–applications of mathematical principles is needed. These components are embedded in the interview form.

Given the significant presence of the RTI model in schools, it is important to fully understand the nature of the model, how specific components of the model are structured by the school, the nature of the assessment processes in place, and the way in which data-based decision making is conducted. The interview form (Form 1) asks for this information. Typically, teachers may not be the best source of all the information. It is suggested that users of the interview form consider asking for this information from relevant school personnel (e.g., principals, instructional specialists, school psychologists, lead teachers). The inclusion of a section of the interview form devoted to RTI is provided for both the areas of reading and mathematics, with an additional question regarding whether an RTI model for behavior is in place. A list of elementary math computational objectives are also included to support the interview process (Form 2).

7

Interviews with teachers should be guided by the need to obtain general information about how they manage instruction and the classroom environment as well as the nature of the strategies already attempted to remediate the problem behavior of the student. Included in the interview is information about the success or failure of these strategies. In addition to, or instead of using a semistructured interviewing form, some evaluators may prefer to be guided by more general questions. This format specifically asks questions around instructional practices, curriculum, assessment, and management. Typically, the interview is conducted following an observation of the teacher teaching the student of interest. The questions in Form 3 are useful to guide this type of interview process.

TEACHER INTERVIEW FORM FOR ACADEMIC PROBLEMS

Student: _____   Teacher: _____

Birth date: _____   Date: _____

Grade: _____   School: _____

Interviewer: _____

GENERAL

Why was this student referred? _____

What type of academic problem(s) does this student have?

_____

READING

Primary type of reading series used

☐ Basal reader

☐ Literature-based

☐ Trade books

Secondary type of reading materials used

☐ Basal reader

☐ Literature-based

☐ Trade books

☐ None

Reading series title (if applicable) _____

    Grade level of series currently placed _____

    Title of book in series currently placed _____

How many groups do you teach? _____

Which group is this student assigned to? _____

At this point in the school year, where is the average student in your class reading?

    Level and book _____

    Place in book (beg., mid., end, specific page) _____

    Time allotted/day for reading _____

How is time divided? (Independent seatwork? Small group? Cooperative groups? Large groups?)

_____

_____

How is placement in reading program determined? _____

_____

How are changes made in the program? _____

_____

_____

Does this student participate in Title I (remedial) reading programs? How much?

_____

_____

Typical daily instructional procedures _____

_____

_____

_____

Contingencies for accuracy? _____

_____

Contingencies for completion? _____

_____

Types of interventions already attempted:

    Simple (e.g., reminders, cues, self-monitoring, motivation, feedback, instructions):

_____

_____

    Moderate (e.g., increasing time of existing instruction, extra tutoring sessions):

_____

_____

    Intensive (e.g., changed curriculum, changed instructional modality, changed instructional grouping, added intensive one-to-one):

_____

_____

Frequency and duration of interventions used:

_____

_____

Extent to which interventions were successful:

_____

_____

Daily scores (if available) for past 2 weeks _____

_____

Group standardized test results (if available) _____

_____

ORAL READING

How does he/she read orally compared to others in his/her reading group?

_____ Much worse   _____ Somewhat worse   _____ About the same

_____ Somewhat better   _____ Much better

In the class?

_____ Much worse   _____ Somewhat worse   _____ About the same

_____ Somewhat better   _____ Much better

WORD ATTACK

Does he/she attempt unknown words? _____

WORD KNOWLEDGE/SIGHT VOCABULARY

How does the student's word knowledge (vocabulary) compare to others in his/her reading group?

_____ Much worse   _____ Somewhat worse   _____ About the same

_____ Somewhat better   _____ Much better

In the class?

_____ Much worse   _____ Somewhat worse   _____ About the same

_____ Somewhat better   _____ Much better

How does the student's sight-word vocabulary compare to others in his/her reading group?

_____ Much worse   _____ Somewhat worse   _____ About the same

_____ Somewhat better   _____ Much better

In the class?

_____ Much worse   _____ Somewhat worse   _____ About the same

_____ Somewhat better   _____ Much better

COMPREHENSION

How well does the student seem to understand what he/she reads compared to others in his/her reading group?

_____ Much worse   _____ Somewhat worse   _____ About the same

_____ Somewhat better   _____ Much better

In the class?

_____ Much worse   _____ Somewhat worse   _____ About the same

_____ Somewhat better   _____ Much better

Areas of comprehension where student has success (+)/difficulty (−):

_____ Main ideas

_____ Prediction

_____ Recollection of facts

_____ Identifying plot

_____ Identifying main characters

_____ Synthesizing the story

_____ Other (describe):

RESPONSE TO INTERVENTION (RTI)—SPECIAL SECTION: READING

Does the school have a currently operating RTI model?

☐ Yes   ☐ No

What type of model (if known) is operating?

☐ Problem solving

☐ Standard protocol

☐ Hybrid

Is this student assigned to tiered instruction beyond Tier 1 for reading?

☐ Yes   ☐ No

For how many years has the model been in place?

☐ Less than 1 year   ☐ 1 year   ☐ 2 years   ☐ 3+ years

How many tiers are in the model?

☐ One   ☐ Two   ☐ Three   ☐ Four or more

What universal screening measures are used for benchmarking?

_____

_____

_____

How often are universal screening measures collected?

☐ One per year   ☐ Two per year   ☐ Three per year   ☐ Four + per year

What measures are being used for progress monitoring?

_____

_____

_____

How often is progress monitoring data collected?

☐ Once per week ☐ Every 2 weeks ☐ Once per month

Other _____

Describe the specific interventions that have been used at each tier.

Tier 1 _____

_____

Tier 2 _____

_____

Tier 3 _____

_____

To which tier is the student currently assigned?

☐ Tier 1 ☐ Tier 2 ☐ Tier 3 ☐ Other _____

What are the benchmark scores (and measures) for the student in the current year?

Fall _____

Winter _____

Spring _____

What are the expected benchmark scores (and measures) for the student in the current year?

Fall _____

Winter _____

Spring _____

What is the student's rate of improvement (ROI) for progress monitoring?

Expected ROI _____

Targeted ROI _____

Attained ROI _____

BEHAVIOR DURING READING

Rate the following areas from 1 to 5 (1 = very unsatisfactory, 3 = satisfactory, 5 = superior).

Reading Group

a. Oral reading ability (as evidenced in reading group) _____

b. Volunteers answers _____

c. When called upon, gives correct answer _____

d. Attends to other students when they read aloud _____

e. Knows the appropriate place in book _____

13

Independent Seatwork

a. Stays on task _____

b. Completes assigned work in required time _____

c. Work is accurate _____

d. Works quietly _____

e. Remains in seat when required _____

Homework (if any)

a. Handed in on time _____

b. Is complete _____

c. Is accurate _____

MATHEMATICS

Curriculum series _____

What are the specific problems in math? _____

_____

Time allotted/day for math _____

How is time divided? (Independent seatwork? Small group? Large group? Cooperative groups?) _____

_____

_____

Are your students grouped in math? _____

If so, how many groups do you have, and in which group is this student placed? _____

_____

For an **average** performing student in your class, at what point in the planned course format would you consider this student at mastery?

(See computational mastery form.) _____

For an **average** performing student in your class, at what point in the planned course format would you consider this student instructional?

(See computational mastery form.) _____

For an **average** performing student in your class, at what point in the planned course format would you consider this student frustrational?

(See computational mastery form.) _____

For the **targeted** student in your class, at what point in the planned course format would you consider this student at mastery?

(See computational mastery form.) _____

For the **targeted** student in your class, at what point in the planned course format would you consider this student instructional?

(See computational mastery form.) _____

For the **targeted** student in your class, at what point in the planned course format would you consider this student frustrational?

(See computational mastery form.) _____

How is mastery assessed? _____

_____

Describe this student's math skills in these critical areas:

Number sense _____

_____

_____

_____

_____

Fluency with whole numbers—addition and subtraction _____

_____

_____

_____

Fluency with whole numbers—multiplication and division _____

_____

_____

_____

Fluency with fractions _____

_____

_____

_____

Geometry _____

_____

_____

_____

Measurement _____

_____

_____

_____

Describe any difficulties this student has in applying math skills in these areas:

Numeration _____

Estimation _____

Time _____

Money_____

Measurement _____

Geometry _____

Graphic display _____

Interpretation of graph _____

Word problems _____

Other _____

How are changes made in the student's math program? _____

_____

Does this student participate in Title I (remedial) math programs? _____

Typical daily instructional procedures _____

_____

_____

Contingencies for accuracy? _____

_____

Contingencies for completion? _____

_____

Types of interventions already attempted:

Simple (e.g., reminders, cues, self-monitoring, motivation, feedback, instructions):

_____

_____

Moderate (e.g., increasing time of existing instruction, extra tutoring sessions):

_____

_____

Intensive (e.g., changed curriculum, changed instructional modality, changed instructional grouping, added intensive one-to-one):

_____

_____

Frequency and duration of interventions used:

_____

_____

Extent to which interventions were successful:

_____

_____

Daily scores (if available) for past 2 weeks _____

_____

Group standardized test results (if available) _____

_____

RESPONSE TO INTERVENTION (RTI)—SPECIAL SECTION: MATH

Does the school have a currently operating RTI model?

□ Yes   □ No

What type of model (if known) is operating?

□ Problem solving

□ Standard protocol

□ Hybrid

Is this student assigned to tiered instruction beyond Tier 1 for math?

□ Yes   □ No

For how many years has the model been in place?

□ Less than 1 year   □ 1 year   □ 2 years   □ 3+ years

How many tiers are in the model?

□ One   □ Two   □ Three   □ Four or more

What universal screening measures are used for benchmarking?

_____

_____

How often are universal screening measures collected?

□ One per year   □ Two per year   □ Three per year   □ Four + per year

What measures are being used for progress monitoring?

_____

_____

How often is progress monitoring data collected?

☐ Once per week ☐ Every 2 weeks ☐ Once per month

Other _____

Describe the specific interventions that have been used at each tier.

Tier 1 _____

_____

Tier 2 _____

_____

Tier 3 _____

_____

To which tier is the student currently assigned?

☐ Tier 1 ☐ Tier 2 ☐ Tier 3 ☐ Other _____

What are the benchmark scores (and measures) for the student in the current year?

Fall _____

Winter _____

Spring _____

What are the expected benchmark scores (and measures) for the student in the current year?

Fall _____

Winter _____

Spring _____

What is the student's rate of improvement (ROI) for progress monitoring?

Expected ROI _____

Targeted ROI _____

Attained ROI _____

BEHAVIOR DURING MATH

Rate the following areas from 1 to 5 (1 = very unsatisfactory, 3 = satisfactory, 5 = superior)

Math Group (large)

a. Volunteers answers _____

b. When called upon, gives correct answer _____

c. Attends to other students when they give answers _____

d. Knows the appropriate place in math book _____

Math Group (small)

a. Volunteers answers _____

b. When called upon, gives correct answer _____

c. Attends to other students when they give answers _____

d. Knows the appropriate place in math book _____

Math Group (cooperative)

a. Volunteers answers _____

b. Contributes to group objectives _____

c. Attends to other students when they give answers _____

d. Facilitates others in group to participate _____

e. Shows appropriate social skills in group _____

Independent Seatwork

a. Stays on task _____

b. Completes assigned work in required time _____

c. Work is accurate _____

d. Works from initial directions _____

e. Works quietly _____

f. Remains in seat when required _____

Homework (if any)

a. Handed in on time _____

b. Is complete _____

c. Is accurate _____

SPELLING

Type of material used for spelling instruction:

☐ Published spelling series

Title of series _____

☐ Basal reading series

Title of series _____

☐ Teacher-made materials _____

☐ Other _____

Level of instruction (if applicable) _____

At this point in the school year, where is the average student in your class spelling?

Level, place in book _____

Time allotted/day for spelling _____

How is time divided? (Independent seatwork? Small group? Cooperative groups?)

_____

_____

How is placement in the spelling program determined? _____

_____

How are changes made in the program? _____

_____

Typical daily instructional procedures _____

_____

Types of interventions already attempted:

Simple (e.g., reminders, cues, self-monitoring, motivation, feedback, instructions):

_____

_____

Moderate (e.g., increasing time of existing instruction, extra tutoring sessions):

_____

_____

Intensive (e.g., changed curriculum, changed instructional modality, changed instructional grouping, added intensive one-to-one):

_____

_____

Frequency and duration of interventions used:

_____

_____

Extent to which interventions were successful:

_____

_____

Contingencies for accuracy? _____

_____

Contingencies for completion? _____

_____

WRITING

Please describe the type of writing assignments you give? _____

_____

Compared to others in your class, does he/she have difficulty with (please provide brief descriptions):

- ☐ Expressing thoughts _____
- ☐ Story length _____
- ☐ Story depth _____
- ☐ Creativity _____

Mechanics:

- ☐ Capitalization
- ☐ Punctuation
- ☐ Grammar
- ☐ Handwriting
- ☐ Spelling

Comments: _____

_____

BEHAVIOR

Are there social–behavioral adjustment problems interfering with this student's academic progress? (be specific)

_____

_____

Check any item that describes this student's behavior:

_____ Distracted, short attention span, unable to concentrate

_____ Hyperactive, constant, aimless movement

_____ Impulsive, aggressive behaviors, lacks self-control

_____ Fluctuating levels of performance

_____ Frequent negative self-statements

_____ Unconsciously repeating verbal or motor acts

_____ Lethargic, sluggish, too quiet

_____ Difficulty sharing or working with others

Does the school have an operating model of RTI for behavior?

☐ Yes   ☐ No

What types of data are collected for monitoring behavioral infractions?

_____

_____

_____

_____

Describe the schoolwide interventions.

_____

_____

_____

_____

Describe the interventions used for Tier 2.

_____

_____

_____

_____

Describe the interventions used for Tier 3.

_____

_____

_____

_____

A COMPUTATION SKILLS MASTERY CURRICULUM

GRADE 1

1. Add two one-digit numbers: sums to 10
2. Subtract two one-digit numbers: combinations to 10

GRADE 2

3. Add two one-digit numbers: sums 11–19
4. Add a one-digit number to a two-digit number—no regrouping
5. Add a two-digit number to a two-digit number—no regrouping
6. Add a three-digit number to a three-digit number—no regrouping
7. Subtract a one-digit number from a one- or two-digit number—combinations to 18
8. Subtract a one-digit number from a two-digit number—no regrouping
9. Subtract a two-digit number from a two-digit number—no regrouping
10. Subtract a three-digit number from a three-digit number—no regrouping
11. Multiplication facts—0's, 1's, 2's

GRADE 3

12. Add three or more one-digit numbers
13. Add three or more two-digit numbers—no regrouping
14. Add three or more three- and four-digit numbers—no regrouping
15. Add a one-digit number to a two-digit number with regrouping
16. Add a two-digit number to a two-digit number with regrouping
17. Add a two-digit number to a three-digit number with regrouping from the 10's column only
18. Add a two-digit number to a three-digit number with regrouping from the 100's column only
19. Add a two-digit number to a three-digit number with regrouping from 10's and 100's columns
20. Add a three-digit number to a three-digit number with regrouping from the 10's column only
21. Add a three-digit number to a three-digit number with regrouping from the 100's column only
22. Add a three-digit number to a three-digit number with regrouping from the 10's and 100's columns
23. Add a four-digit number to a four-digit number with regrouping in one to three columns
24. Subtract two four-digit numbers—no regrouping
25. Subtract a one-digit number from a two-digit number with regrouping
26. Subtract a two-digit number from a two-digit number with regrouping
27. Subtract a two-digit number from a three-digit number with regrouping from the 10's column only
28. Subtract a two-digit number from a three-digit number with regrouping from the 100's column only
29. Subtract a two-digit number from a three-digit number with regrouping from the 10's and 100's columns
30. Subtract a three-digit number from a three-digit number with regrouping from the 10's column only
31. Subtract a three-digit number from a three-digit number with regrouping from the 100's column only

32. Subtract a three-digit number from a three-digit number with regrouping from the 10's and 100's columns
33. Multiplication facts—3–9

GRADE 4

34. Add a five- or six-digit number to a five- or six-digit number with regrouping in any column
35. Add three or more two-digit numbers with regrouping
36. Add three or more three-digit numbers with regrouping
37. Subtract a five- or six-digit number from a five- or six-digit number with regrouping in any column
38. Multiply a two-digit number by a one-digit number with no regrouping
39. Multiply a three-digit number by a one-digit number with no regrouping
40. Multiply a two-digit number by a one-digit number with no regrouping
41. Multiply a three-digit number by a one-digit number with regrouping
42. Division facts—0–9
43. Divide a two-digit number by a one-digit number with no remainder
44. Divide a two-digit number by a one-digit number with remainder
45. Divide a three-digit number by a one-digit number with remainder
46. Divide a four-digit number by a one-digit number with remainder

GRADE 5

47. Multiply a two-digit number by a two-digit number with regrouping
48. Multiply a three-digit number by a two-digit number with regrouping
49. Multiply a three-digit number by a three-digit number with regrouping

QUESTIONS TO GUIDE GENERAL TEACHER INTERVIEWS FOR ACADEMIC SKILLS

Teacher _____   Student _____

Academic subject(s) _____   Date _____

1. What was the specific instructional assignment being taught during the observation?

2. How was the instructional assignment presented to the student?

3. What opportunities were presented for guided practice?

4. What opportunities were presented for independent practice?

5. What opportunities were presented for feedback to students?

6. What were the specific objectives of the instructional lesson observed?

7. How did you determine whether the student was successful during the lesson observed?

8. What type of additional support beyond your normal classroom instruction does this student need to succeed?

9. What strategies seem to work with this student?

10. What strategies do not seem to work with this student?

11. What types of assessment information do you collect?

12. How do you use the information gathered about student performance?

13. During group instruction, what clues do you use to evaluate a student's performance?

14. What adaptations do you make or permit on assignments?

15. What adaptations do you make or permit on tests?

16. What kind of support can you expect from supervisors and administrators for more intensive intervention changes if they are needed?

Many thanks to Christine Schubel, EdS, for her contributions to this form.

Academic Performance Rating Scale

ANOTHER APPROACH TO GATHERING INFORMATION about student academic performance and classroom structure is to use a teacher rating scale. DuPaul, Rapport, and Perriello (1991) developed the Academic Performance Rating Scale (Form 4), designed to provide teacher-based ratings of student performance in math and language arts among students in grades 1–6. The factor analysis of the scale results in three subscales: Academic Success, Impulse Control, and Academic Productivity (as judged by the teacher) (see Table 1). Normative data divided by gender, along with instructions for scoring for each factor, are provided (see Table 2). Note that items 12, 13, 15, 16, 17, 18, and 19 are reversed scored (i.e., 5 = 1; 4 = 2; 3 = 3; 2 = 4; 1 = 5), so that the total higher scores always reflect more desirable outcomes.

ACADEMIC PERFORMANCE RATING SCALE*

Student _____ Date _____

Age _____ Grade _____ Teacher _____

For each of the items below, please estimate the above student's performance over the PAST WEEK.
For each item, please circle one choice only.

1. Estimate the percentage of written **math work** completed (regardless of accuracy) relative to classmates.	0–49% 0 pt	50–69% 2	70–79% 3	80–89% 4	90–100% 5
2. Estimate the percentage of written **language arts** work completed (regardless of accuracy) relative to classmates.	0–49% 1	50–69% 2	70–79% 3	80–89% 4	90–100% 5
3. Estimate the accuracy of completed written **math** work (i.e., percent correct of work done).	0–64% 1	65–69% 2	70–79% 3	80–89% 4	90–100% 5
4. Estimate the accuracy of completed written **language arts** work (i.e., percent correct of work done).	0–64% 1	65–69% 2	70–79% 3	80–89% 4	90–100% 5
5. How consistent has the quality of this child's academic work been over the past week?	Consistently poor 1	More poor than successful 2	Variable 3	More successful than poor 4	Consistently successful 5
6. How frequently does the student accurately follow teacher instructions and/or class discussion during *large-group* (e.g., whole-class) instruction?	Never 1	Rarely 2	Sometimes 3	Often 4	Very often 5
7. How frequently does the student accurately follow teacher instructions and/or class discussion during *small-group* (e.g., reading group) instruction?	Never 1	Rarely 2	Sometimes 3	Often 4	Very often 5

From DuPaul, Rapport, and Perriello (1991, pp. 299–300). Copyright 1991 by the National Association of School Psychologists. Reprinted by permission of the publisher. *www.nasponline.org*.

8. How quickly does the child learn new material (i.e., pick up novel concepts)?	Very slowly 1	Slowly 2	Average 3	Quickly 4	Very quickly 5
9. What is the quality or neatness of this child's handwriting?	Poor 1	Fair 2	Average 3	Above average 4	Excellent 5
10. What is the quality of this child's reading skills?	Poor 1	Fair 2	Average 3	Above average 4	Excellent 5
11. What is the quality of this child's writing skills?	Poor 1	Fair 2	Average 3	Above average 4	Excellent 5
12. How often does the child complete written work in a careless, hasty fashion?	Never 1	Rarely 2	Sometimes 3	Often 4	Very often 5
13. How frequently does the child take more time to complete work than his/her classmates?	Never 1	Rarely 2	Sometimes 3	Often 4	Very often 5
14. How often is the child able to pay attention without your prompting him/her?	Never 1	Rarely 2	Sometimes 3	Often 4	Very often 5
15. How frequently does this child require your assistance to accurately complete his/her academic work?	Never 1	Rarely 2	Sometimes 3	Often 4	Very often 5
16. How often does the child begin written work prior to understanding the directions?	Never 5	Rarely 4	Sometimes 3	Often 2	Very often 1
17. How frequently does this child have difficulty recalling material from a previous day's lessons?	Never 5	Rarely 4	Sometimes 3	Often 2	Very often 1
18. How often does the child appear to be staring excessively or "spaced out"?	Never 5	Rarely 4	Sometimes 3	Often 2	Very often 1
19. How often does the child appear withdrawn or tend to lack an emotional response in a social situation?	Never 5	Rarely 4	Sometimes 3	Often 2	Very often 1

APRS SCORING INSTRUCTIONS:

Step 1: Write in the score assigned by the teacher for each item in the blank column.

Step 2: Sum the columns and write the total in the last row.

Item #	Academic Success	Impulse Control	Academic Productivity
1			
2			
3			
4			
5			
6			
7			
8			
9			
10			
11			
12**			
13**			
14			
15**			
16**			
17**			
18**			
19**			
TOTALS	Academic Success score	Impulse Control score	Academic Productivity score

---

**These items have been reversed scored.

30

TABLE 1. Factor Structure of the Academic Performance Rating Scale (APRS)

Scale item	Academic Success	Impulse Control	Academic Productivity
1. Math work completed	.30	−.02	**.84**
2. Language arts completed	.32	.06	**.82**
3. Math work accuracy	**.68**	.17	**.50**
4. Language arts accuracy	**.68**	.17	**.50**
5. Consistency of work	**.50**	.21	**.72**
6. Follows group instructions	.41	.35	**.69**
7. Follows small-group instructions	.39	.37	**.64**
8. Learns material quickly	**.81**	.17	.39
9. Neatness of handwriting	.41	**.50**	.31
10. Quality of reading	**.87**	.16	.23
11. Quality of speaking	**.80**	.20	.21
12. Careless work completion	.15	**.72**	.36
13. Time to complete work	.36	.21	**.61**
14. Attention without prompts	.24	.35	**.53**
15. Requires assistance	.44	.39	**.53**
16. Begins work carelessly	.16	**.82**	.02
17. Recalls difficulties	**.66**	.35	.38
18. Stares excessively	.19	**.39**	.67
19. Social withdrawal	.16	**.28**	.57
Estimate of % variance	55.5	**6.6**	6.1

Note. Boldface values indicate items included in the factor named in the column head. From DuPaul, Rapport, and Perriello (1991, p. 290). Copyright 1991 by the National Association of School Psychologists. Reprinted by permission of the publisher. *www.nasponline.org.*

TABLE 2. Means and Standard Deviations for the APRS by Grade and Gender

Grade/Gender	Total score	Academic Success	Impulse Control	Academic Productivity
Grade 1 ($n = 82$)				
Girls ($n = 40$)	67.02 (16.27)	23.92 (7.37)	9.76 (2.49)	44.68 (10.91)
Boys ($n = 42$)	71.95 (16.09)	26.86 (6.18)	10.67 (2.82)	46.48 (11.24)
Grade 2 ($n = 91$)				
Girls ($n = 46$)	72.56 (12.33)	26.61 (5.55)	10.15 (2.70)	47.85 (7.82)
Boys ($n = 45$)	67.84 (14.86)	25.24 (6.15)	9.56 (2.72)	44.30 (10.76)
Grade 3 ($n = 95$)				
Girls ($n = 46$)	72.10 (14.43)	25.07 (6.07)	10.86 (2.65)	47.88 (9.35)
Boys ($n = 49$)	68.49 (16.96)	25.26 (6.53)	9.27 (2.67)	45.61 (11.89)
Grade 4 ($n = 79$)				
Girls ($n = 38$)	67.79 (18.69)	24.08 (7.56)	10.36 (2.91)	44.26 (11.96)
Boys ($n = 41$)	69.77 (15.83)	25.35 (6.50)	9.83 (2.77)	45.71 (10.22)
Grade 5 ($n = 79$)				
Girls ($n = 44$)	73.02 (14.10)	26.11 (6.01)	10.76 (2.34)	48.36 (9.05)
Boys ($n = 35$)	63.68 (18.04)	23.14 (7.31)	8.69 (2.82)	42.40 (12.47)
Grade 6 ($n = 70$)				
Girls ($n = 31$)	74.10 (14.45)	26.59 (6.26)	10.79 (2.25)	48.77 (9.13)
Boys ($n = 39$)	65.24 (12.39)	23.75 (5.90)	9.05 (2.35)	43.59 (8.19)

Note. Standard deviations are in parentheses. From DuPaul, Rapport, and Perriello (1991, p. 291). Copyright 1991 by the National Association of School Psychologists. Reprinted by permission of the publisher. *www.nasponline. org.*

Student Interview

It is important in the process of academic assessment to determine how the student being assessed perceives the demands of the academic environment. This information is best obtained through an interview of the student. Specifically, questions should cover the following areas: the degree to which the student understands directions of assignments; the degree of success predicted by the student on each assignment; the student's perception of how much time he/she is given by the teacher to complete assignments; the student's knowledge of how to seek assistance when experiencing difficulty; and the student's understanding of the consequences of not completing academic work. This information can be obtained by means of a semistructured interview, conducted immediately after an observation of the student engaged in an assigned task. A simple format with general guidelines is provided for conducting the interview (Form 5).

STUDENT INTERVIEW FORM

Student name _____

Subject _____

Date _____

STUDENT-REPORTED BEHAVIOR

_____ None completed for this area

Understands expectations of teacher	☐ Yes	☐ No	☐ Not sure
Understands assignments	☐ Yes	☐ No	☐ Not sure
Feels he/she can do the assignments	☐ Yes	☐ No	☐ Not sure
Likes the subject	☐ Yes	☐ No	☐ Not sure
Feels he/she is given enough time to complete assignments	☐ Yes	☐ No	☐ Not sure
Feels like he/she is called upon to participate in discussions	☐ Yes	☐ No	☐ Not sure

General comments:

Questions used to guide interview:

Do you think you are pretty good in _____?

If you had to pick one thing about _____ you liked, what would it be?

If you had to pick one thing about _____ you don't like, what would it be?

What do you do when you are unable to solve a problem or answer a question with your assignment in _____?

Do you enjoy working with other students when you are having trouble with your assignment in _____?

Does the teacher call on you too often? Not often enough? In _____?

Direct Observation:
Manual for the Behavioral Observation
of Students in Schools (BOSS)

SYSTEMATICALLY OBSERVING STUDENTS IN CLASSROOMS is an essential part of the assessment of the instructional environment. This is true whether the referral problem is not completing assignments, having difficulties in reading, or being unable to quickly and accurately compute addition facts.

Although learning to conduct systematic observations is not difficult, it does take some concentrated practice and effort to master the method. It is a rare person (if such a person exists) who can put on a pair of skis for the first time and go schussing down the slopes of Killington. It is a rare person who can pick up a basketball and make four consecutive three-pointers. It is a rare person who can sit down at a piano for the first time and play popular songs. It is a rare person who can get in front of a group of third-grade children and teach subtraction with regrouping. Attaining the skills to be a good skier, a good athlete, a good pianist, or a good teacher takes practice. Learning these skills requires studying persons who are considered experts at the skills in question, trying out the new skills under supervision of such experts, receiving feedback regarding one's performance, and then practicing the newly learned skills.

This manual describes the rationale and process of direct observation. In particular, the use of the BOSS, a measure designed specifically for direct observation of academic skills, is presented.

Many thanks to Mark Fugate, PhD, for suggestions and contributions to the development of the first edition of this section of the workbook.

RATIONALE

Systematic direct observation is defined as a form of quantitative data collection. Its main purpose is the numerical recording of behaviors occurring in the observational setting. For example, if Roberta is reported as not paying attention, systematic observation may show that she was off-task 50% of the time. If Jason is reported as not completing his work, than systematic observation may find that, on average, Jason completes only two of five in-class math assignments per day. If Miguel is reported as fighting on the playground at recess, systematic observation may reveal that he was sent to the principal for fighting five times in the past 2 weeks. In each case, the use of systematic observation is an attempt to capture the quantitative aspects of the behavior taking place.

Of course, teachers and other professionals are constantly observing children in schools; this form of observation provides a subjective impression of a child's behavior. These impressions are important and meaningful, and can be viewed as helpful data in making sense of a child's classroom behavior. Unfortunately, although these subjective impressions are frequently accurate, they can also be inaccurate. For example, Marcus may be reported by a teacher to be a disruptive and "nasty" child due to his frequent teasing of peers. Such a report suggests that the behavior occurs frequently and should be easily observable. If asked to complete a rating scale that includes items about teasing, the teacher may report that the behavior occurs often, when, in reality, the behavior may occur rarely. However, the fact that the behavior is viewed as negative and obnoxious by the teacher may make it seem much worse than it really is. Another teacher may report that Jamie is off-task "all the time." Certainly, although Jamie's off-task behavior may be frequent, it is unlikely that she is off-task all the time. Using a form of systematic observation makes it possible to describe the teasing or off-task occasions objectively, in terms of their frequency. Of course, even a low frequency of misbehavior can be very troubling; teasing that occurs once per week may be viewed as out of line and needing to be stopped. However, knowing that the problem is not as severe as one first thought may be very important in deciding how to best perceive the problem. Systematic observation of Jamie may reveal that she is actually off-task at the same rate as her peers. If that is the case, why does the teacher perceive her to have such a high frequency of inattentiveness? Using systematic observation one can report, in a more definitive way, the nature of the off-task behavior that has led the teacher to develop such a perception.

There are several important reasons for conducting systematic observations. First, as already noted, getting subjective opinions about behavior is important, because these perceptions represent how persons who deal with the problem experience it; indeed, they form the basis of what we think is going on. However, subjective perceptions need to be systematically confirmed or disconfirmed. In addition, as suggested earlier, the problem may be either less or more severe than originally indicated. Thus, two important reasons for conducting systematic observation are the need to confirm or disconfirm subjective reports and to determine the exact severity of the reported problem.

A third important reason for conducting systematic observation is to provide a baseline or benchmark against which to assess the success or failure of an instructional intervention. Whenever changes in behavior occur, it is important to document the relative impact of the intervention by comparing the student's present performance with his/her performance prior to the intervention. This comparison allows the teacher, the student, and the parents to see the gains (or losses) in performance that have occurred over time. It is also required in some states that such baseline data be obtained as part of the evaluation process.

A final reason to collect systematic observation data is to provide feedback to parties (parents, students, teachers, and other school professionals) regarding the types and levels of problems students are currently having. By using systematic observation, interested persons can actually see how behavior is changing in the classroom. Indeed, in the evaluation of students being considered for eligibility as having a specific learning disability, current law requires that observational data be collected that reflect student behavior in their learning environment, including the general education classroom. Systematic observation, as described here, would easily meet this requirement.

IDENTIFYING THE BEHAVIORS FOR OBSERVATION

Systematic observation requires that the behaviors to be observed be carefully and precisely defined. Behaviors that are defined too broadly may be difficult to observe accurately. At the same time, behaviors defined too narrowly may not be meaningful units of responding. The key to effectively identifying behaviors for observation is to think about which ones are likely to be the most relevant to the problem(s) of interest in the classroom.

The literature has suggested that when the problem is in the area of academics, the observation of *student academic engaged time* is a critical variable. Strong and significant relationships have been identified between high levels of academic engagement and successful academic performance. The relationships suggest a need for a careful analysis of the types of engagement and nonengagement that students exhibit in classrooms (see Chapter 2 of *Academic Skills Problems, Fourth Edition*, for a more detailed discussion).

The BOSS includes two categories of engagement and three categories of nonengagement. An additional category, which examines the types of instruction occurring in the classroom, is also included in the code. When the interaction of the student's engaged and nonengaged time is examined, a clear picture of the student's behavior in a context of meaningful academic outcomes can be obtained.

USE OF TECHNOLOGY
IN CONDUCTING SYSTEMATIC OBSERVATION

Computer and digital technology has advanced significantly to make the process of conducting systematic observations easier and much more convenient. In particular, the use of personal digital assistants (PDAs) and smartphone devices has become increasingly popular. These handheld devices offer substantial advantages in the collection of systematic observational data. Included in the PDA or smartphone is a timing device, a cueing device, a data storage system, and a data analysis system. The handheld device offers an opportunity to be somewhat unobtrusive in the observation process—an important consideration when observing students during academic endeavors. In addition, because of the use of syncing capability, information collected on a handheld device can be automatically transferred to a personal computer.

Several software programs have been developed to facilitate the collection of systematic observations. Currently, most of these are available for data collection on a PDA or laptop computer. Development of similar programs for smartphones is likely to emerge over the next few years. Each of the programs offers somewhat different features, and potential users are cautioned to examine the products to find out which ones best meet their needs. Products that are currently available include the !Observe program (*www.psycsoft.com*), the Behavior Assessment System for Children–2 Portable Observation System (BASC POP; *www.pearsonassessments. com*), Behavior Tracker Pro (*www.BehaviorTrackerPro.com*), and the BOSS (*www.pearsonassessments.com*). The programs have different features and degrees of flexibility. In particular, the POP is tied somewhat to the observational system built into the BASC-2, but it does enable users to customize the observation to their own behavioral codes. The !Observe system is a fully customized system and not linked to any particular observation code. Likewise, the Behavior Tracker Pro is currently the only smartphone-based application, but it is designed primarily for obtaining frequency and duration data. The program is particularly useful for collecting data for a functional behavioral assessment.

In contrast to these codes, the BOSS software is based primarily on collecting data in academic settings and derives the specific codes for observation from research that specifies the importance of types and nature of engaged and nonengaged academic student behaviors. The code does contain some capacity for user-defined codes, although the number of codes is somewhat limited. More important, the BOSS code, unlike other software, allows prompting of the observer through multiple modalities, has a built-in feature for collecting data on a peer comparison student, and uses a system of data collection that mixes momentary and partial-interval data collection that has strong research support. An important consideration that users must understand is that these programs were developed for use with PDAs running on the Palm OS platform. Given the developments of smartphone technology over the past several years, users would have to locate older handheld devices to run these programs. It is anticipated that over the next few years, many of these applications currently running on the Palm OS platforms will be reconfigured to operate on smartphones.

A detailed description of the paper-and-pencil version of the BOSS is provided in this manual. All features of the paper-and-pencil version are also included within the software. In addition, the software provides room for user-defined codes that are not part of the paper-and-pencil version. Features of the BOSS software are also presented. Plans for a smartphone-based application of the BOSS are under development at the time this volume was published, with anticipation of the product availability sometime in the next 2 years.

GUIDELINES FOR PAPER-AND-PENCIL DIRECT OBSERVATION

Materials

- Two sharp pencils or fine-point pens.
- Clipboard
- Timing device: An interval audiotape or digital recording with a tape player or digital player and earpiece (or headphones). A stopwatch is not recommended, since it can be difficult to attend both to the watch and to events in the classroom. In addition, keeping track of the interval in which the observation is taking place is critical. Use of an audio-cueing device allows the observer to maintain vigilance to the classroom while simultaneously recording with accuracy.
- BOSS coding sheet(s) permitting up to 30 minutes of observation. Each minute is divided into four intervals of 15 seconds each. An observation sheet is provided for use with the BOSS, consisting of 180 intervals (60 per page) for a total of 45 minutes (Form 6).

Classroom Manners

- Before observing in a classroom, the observer will need to become familiar with the daily schedule, routine, and physical layout of the classroom.
- The observer should meet briefly with the teacher before the observation to learn about classroom rules or procedures that may be in effect during the observation.
- The observer should ask the teacher the best place to sit or stand, so as to be able to observe the target student directly.
- The observer needs to have a clear view of the student, but should not be too obtrusive, and should be sure to stay out of major traffic areas for other students.
- During the observation, the teacher should teach as he/she normally does.
- The observer should minimize any interactions with students or the teacher during the observation period.
- The teacher should not introduce the observer to the class when he/she arrives, but should be instructed to tell the students (prior to the observer's arrival) that someone will be coming to observe what goes on in the classroom.
- If the assessment includes working individually with the target student, it is recommended that the direct observation be conducted before the observer meets individually with the student.
- The observer's entrance into the classroom should be as naturalistic as possible. It can help if he/she enters the classroom during a natural break in the instructional routine.

MAKING A CODING INTERVAL RECORDING

Making an audio recording to use for cueing during observations is not difficult, but it does take a little time. A cueing recording for the BOSS should be at least 30 minutes in length and contain intervals of 15 seconds.

Generate a recording by naming aloud the intervals. Using a stopwatch and a tape recorder, the observer simply states the necessary intervals. Each interval is cued by saying, "Observe 1," "Observe 2," "Observe 3," and so forth, as each interval passes. Using the word *observe* before each number provides a cue that signals when the interval is about to begin. A brief statement should also be provided prior to beginning the first observation interval, such as, "Get ready to observe." As the last interval on the recording ends, the observer should add an ending statement, such as "End of observation," or some other appropriate closing comment.

An advantage of saying aloud the intervals is that it provides a cue immediately before each momentary time sample observation must be made. Preparing the recording can be tedious, and if concentration is not maintained, accuracy of the recording may be compromised (i.e., each interval may not be 15 seconds in length).

Another option in developing the audio recording is simply to cue each observation interval with a specific sound (i.e., a "beep"). If the observer uses this method, it may be valuable once each minute to state the interval number, in case the observer loses track of the interval.

An advantage of the BOSS software is that the timing device is built into the PDA. Once the user specifies the interval length to be used, the PDA device will beep at each designated interval. In addition, a counter is provided that displays both the interval number and the elapsed seconds since the observations began. The loudness of the sound can be easily controlled, and for those PDAs equipped with a "vibrate" option, it is possible for the cueing device to be silent. This is an important feature if the observer is concerned about any potential distraction to students during observation. Likewise, the use of a PDA device to conduct the observation removes the need for a digital recorder, earphone, clipboard, and other more obtrusive materials.

COMPLETING IDENTIFYING INFORMATION

The coding sheet used with the BOSS (Form 6) is included at the end of this section of the workbook. At the top of the BOSS coding sheet, the observer should be sure to write in the child's name, date, his/her own name, and the subject matter being observed. In addition, the observer is asked to note the type of instructional setting observed. The time of the observation, along with the length of the observation intervals, should also be recorded. If using the BOSS software, the user is able to set the interval length from 3 to 60 seconds, as well as the nature of the cue (low beep, high beep, vibration, or flash). The type of setting is also indicated on the BOSS software.

- *ISW:TPsnt (student in independent seatwork, teacher present).* In this setting, the student is doing independent seatwork while the teacher is available to assist individual children. Typically, the teacher is circulating around the room.
- *ISW:TSmGP (student in independent seatwork, teacher in small group not including target student).* This setting is marked when the target student is engaged in independent seatwork and the teacher is working with a small group that *does not* include the target student.
- *SmGp:Tled (student in small group led by teacher).* This setting is marked when the target student is in a small group (defined as eight or fewer students) that is led by the teacher.
- *LgGp:Tled (student in large group led by teacher).* This setting is marked when the target student is in a large group (defined as more than eight students) that is led by the teacher.
- *Other.* When "Other" is used, the type of instructional setting should be noted in the margin.

The classroom setting is marked by circling the appropriate designation. If the instructional activity changes during the course of the observation, this change should be noted on the observation form by circling the interval where the change occurred and writing in the type of setting that is now in place. All of these same data are also recorded in the opening screens of the BOSS software (see Figure 3).

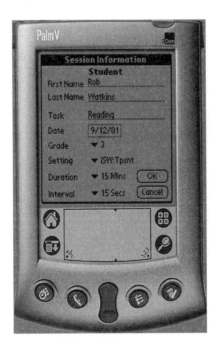

FIGURE 3. Screen from the BOSS software showing session information.

OBSERVING PEER COMPARISON STUDENTS

A behavioral observation is more meaningful if the target student's behavior is compared to the same behaviors displayed by peers. The BOSS requires that data be collected not only on the target student but also on peers in the same classroom. As noted on the BOSS observation form, every fifth interval is shaded. During each of these intervals, observations are conducted on a randomly selected peer rather than the target student. Before beginning the observation, the observer should decide the sequence of peer comparison observations. For example, the observer may decide to start in the front left of the classroom and observe a different peer each fifth interval, moving down the row and then from back to front. In truth, it does not matter in which order the peer comparison data are collected. It does help, however, for the observer to have an observation plan thought out before beginning the observation of the target student.

Data from intervals in which different peers were observed are combined to derive a peer comparison score for each of the behaviors.

In the BOSS software, the peer comparison data-collection process is facilitated by both an audio and visual cue that indicates to the observer that the peer should be observed. Every fifth interval, a slightly different sound occurs, and the screen flashes to a slightly different version, which is marked as the peer observation data. These cues occur automatically, and the data for the peer comparison student are calculated independently from those of the targeted student.

CODING ACADEMIC ENGAGEMENT

The BOSS divides academic engagement into two subcategories: active or passive engaged time. In either case, the student is considered to be on-task. Each of these behaviors is recorded as a momentary time sample. At the beginning of each cued interval, the observer looks at the targeted student; determines whether the student is on-task; and, if so, whether the on-task behavior constitutes an active or passive form of engagement, as defined below. The occurrence of the behavior at that moment is recorded by making a mark in the appropriate box on the scoring sheet. If using the BOSS software, the observer simply touches the appropriate button (see Figure 4).

Active Engaged Time

Active engaged time (AET) is defined as those times when the student is actively attending to the assigned work. Examples of AET include the following:

- Writing.
- Reading aloud.
- Raising a hand.
- Talking to the teacher about the assigned material.
- Talking to a peer about the assigned material.
- Looking up a word in a dictionary.

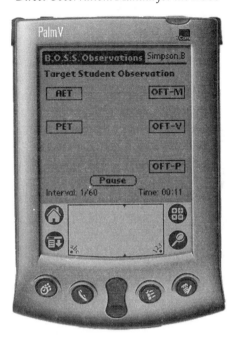

FIGURE 4. Screen from the BOSS software showing the observation screen.

AET *should not* be scored if the student is:

- Talking about nonacademic material (Verbal Off-Task).
- Walking to the worksheet bin (Motor Off-Task).
- Calling out (Verbal Off-Task), unless it is considered an appropriate response style for that classroom.
- Aimlessly flipping the pages of a book (Motor Off-Task).
- Any other form of off-task behavior.

Passive Engaged Time

Passive engaged time (PET) is defined as those times when the student is passively attending to assigned work. Examples of PET include the following:

- Listening to a lecture.
- Looking at an academic worksheet.
- Reading assigned material silently.
- Looking at the blackboard during teacher instruction.
- Listening to a peer respond to a question.

PET *should not* be scored if the student is:

- Aimlessly looking around the classroom (Passive Off-Task).
- Silently reading unassigned material (Passive Off-Task).
- Any other form of off-task behavior.

At times it may be difficult to determine immediately whether the child is passively engaged or daydreaming at the first moment of an interval. In this case, it is appropriate to code PET if it becomes apparent later during that interval that the student was indeed passively engaged.

CODING NONENGAGEMENT

When a student is not engaged in academic behavior, three possible categories of off-task behavior are coded. These behaviors are recorded using a partial-interval observation method. If any of the three behaviors occurs at any point during the interval, a mark is made in the appropriate box. Multiple occurrences of the same behavior within a single interval are noted only one time. If using the BOSS software, the appropriate buttons on the screen are touched.

Off-Task Motor

Off-task motor behaviors (OFT-M) are defined as any instance of motor activity that is not directly associated with an assigned academic task. Examples of OFT-M include the following:

- Engaging in any out-of-seat behavior (defined as buttocks not in contact with the seat).
- Aimlessly flipping the pages of a book.
- Manipulating objects not related to the academic task (e.g., playing with a paper clip, throwing paper, twirling a pencil, folding paper).
- Physically touching another student when not related to an academic task.
- Bending or reaching, such as picking up a pencil off the floor.
- Drawing or writing that is not related to an assigned academic activity.
- Turning around in one's seat, orienting away from the classroom instruction.
- Fidgeting in one's seat (i.e., engaging in repetitive motor movements for at least 3 consecutive seconds; student must be off-task for this category to be scored).

OFT-M *should not* be scored if the student is:

- Passing paper to a student, as instructed by the teacher.
- Coloring on an assigned worksheet, as instructed (AET).
- Laughing at a joke told by another student (Off-Task Verbal).
- Swinging feet while working on assigned material (AET or PET).

Off-Task Verbal

Off-task verbal behaviors (OFT-V) are defined as any audible verbalizations that are not permitted and/or are not related to an assigned academic task. Examples of OFT-V include the following:

- Making any audible sound, such as whistling, humming, or forced burping.
- Talking to another student about issues unrelated to an assigned academic task.
- Talking to another student about an assigned academic task when such talk is prohibited by the teacher.
- Making unauthorized comments or remarks.
- Calling out answers to academic problems when the teacher has not specifically asked for an answer or permitted such behavior.

OFT-V *should not* be scored if the student is:

- Laughing at a joke told by the teacher.
- Talking to another student about the assigned academic work during a cooperative learning group (AET).
- Calling out the answer to a problem when the teacher has permitted such behavior during instruction (AET).

Off-Task Passive

Off-task passive behaviors (OFT-P) are defined as those times when a student is passively not attending to an assigned academic activity for a period of at least 3 consecutive seconds. Included are those times when a student is quietly waiting after the completion of an assigned task but is not engaged in an activity authorized by the teacher. Examples of OFT-P behavior include the following:

- Sitting quietly in an unassigned activity.
- Looking around the room.
- Staring out the window.
- Passively listening to other students talk about issues unrelated to the assigned academic activity.

It is important to note that the student must be passively off-task for 3-consecutive seconds *within an interval* to be scored. Should the interval end before the full 3-second period occurs, OFT-P is not scored for that interval, and a new consecutive 3-second period is required for the next interval. For instance, suppose a student begins to stare out the window during the third interval of observation. The observer counts only 2 seconds before the fourth interval begins. The student continues to stare out the window for over 3 seconds in this interval. In this case, only the fourth interval would be scored for OFT-P. If the student had stopped staring out the window after 2 seconds of the fourth interval, then OFT-P *should not* have been scored for either interval. In addition, OFT-P *should not* be scored if the student is:

- Quietly reading an assigned book (PET).
- Passively listening to other students talk about the assigned work in a cooperative learning group (PET).

CODING TEACHER-DIRECTED INSTRUCTION

Teacher-directed instruction (TDI) is coded every fifth interval, again by means of a partial-interval observation method. The purpose of these observations is to provide a sampling of time in which the teacher is actively engaged in direct instruction of the classroom. TDI is defined as those times when the teacher is directly instructing the class or individuals within the class. Examples of TDI include times when the teacher is:

- Instructing the whole class or group.
- Demonstrating academic material at the board.
- Individually assisting a student with an assigned task.

TDI should not be scored if the teacher is:

- Scolding the class or an individual student for misbehavior.
- Giving instructions for an academic activity.
- Sitting at his/her desk grading papers.
- Speaking to an individual student or the class about nonacademic issues.

REVIEW: PROCEDURE FOR CONDUCTING THE OBSERVATION

After the observer is seated in the classroom, he/she begins the observation by starting the recording or touching the start button on the screen, if using the BOSS software. The observer is cued with the words "Observe one" if using the recording, or an audible beep or vibration if using the PDA. Using the number word to indicate the beginning of each interval or the cue from the PDA, the observer immediately records whether the student is actively or passively engaged in academic behavior. If the student is off-task at the moment that the word *one* was heard or the cue occurred, the observer leaves the boxes blank or does not touch either the AET or PET buttons. For the remainder of the interval, the observer watches to see if the student engages in any form of off-task behavior. Before the next interval begins, if the student gets out of his/her seat and then talks to another student about nonacademic issues, marks would be made in the OFT-M and OFT-V columns of interval one, or these buttons on the screen would be pushed. The BOSS software darkens the color of the button once pushed, until the interval ends. If the observer makes an error within the interval, he/she simply pushes the button again and the recording is erased. Any buttons darkened at the end of an interval are recorded in the database. The process is repeated until the observer reaches interval 5. Having decided to start with the students in the first row of desks for purposes of peer comparison data collection, upon hearing the words "Observe five" or the peer comparison cue, the observer now looks to see whether the student sitting in the first row, left side of the room, is on-task. That student is now observed for any off-task behavior throughout the remainder of the interval. In addition, during the fifth interval, the observer records whether the teacher engaged in any directed instruction. When the sixth interval begins, the observer returns to watching and recording the behavior of the target student. This process is repeated until the observation is completed. Figure 5 displays a completed sample observation using the BOSS, and Figure 6 shows a report output for the same observation from the BOSS software.

SCORING THE BOSS

All categories of the BOSS are scored using the same metric: percentage of intervals in which the behavior occurred. Hand scoring requires that the number of intervals in which the behavior was marked as occurring be divided by the total number of intervals of observing the student, and multiplying the result by 100.

- **Step 1:** Add the number of times each behavior occurred for the target student *only*, across the rows. Enter this number on the data-collection sheet in the corresponding cell under the column marked "S" (for target student). Be sure *not* to add the number of occurrences in the intervals in which peer comparison data were collected (see Figure 7).

As can be seen in Figure 7, the target student was observed to have engaged in AET for 5 out of the first 15 intervals observed, PET for 5, OFT-M for 2, OFT-V for 3, and OFT-P for 3.

- **Step 2:** Add up the number of intervals each behavior is observed for the target student across the entire observation, and record the total in the lower left portion of the form. This is done by simply adding the "S" row totals for each behavior.
- **Step 3:** Determine the total number of intervals in which the target student was observed and record this number in the space provided in the lower left portion of the data collection sheet. Again, be sure to eliminate any intervals in which the peer comparison data were collected.

As evident in Figure 5, the target student was observed for a total of 48 intervals during this observation.

- **Step 4:** Divide the number of occurrences of each behavior by the total intervals observed and multiply by 100. This is the percentage of intervals in which the behavior was observed to occur. Record this percentage in the spaces provided.
- **Step 5:** Repeat this process, but now calculate only the intervals in which peer comparison data (P) were collected. Eliminate any intervals in which the target student was observed (see Figure 8).
- **Step 6:** Repeat the process one more time, but now examine only the intervals in which TDI data were collected (see Figure 9). Eliminate any intervals in which the target student data were collected. Note that the intervals in which peer comparison data were collected are the same ones in which TDI is observed.

BEHAVIORAL OBSERVATION OF STUDENTS IN SCHOOLS (BOSS)

Child Observed: __Justin__   Academic Subject: __Math__

Date: __9/15/09__   Setting: _____ ISW:TPsnt __X__   _____ SmGp:TPsnt

Observer: __JGL__   _____ ISW:TSmGp   _____ LgGp:TPsnt

Time of Observation: __10:30__   Interval Length: __15__   Other: _____

Moment	1	2	3	4	5*	6	7	8	9	10*	11	12	13	14	15*	S	P	T
AET	\		\		\	\	\			\		\				5	2	
PET		\						\	\		\			\	\	5	1	
Partial																		
OFT-M	\								\						\	2	1	
OFT-V						\	\			\	\					3	1	
OFT-P	\			\	\								\			3	1	
TDI															\			1

Moment	16	17	18	19	20*	21	22	23	24	25*	26	27	28	29	30*	S	P	T
AET	\			\							\				\	3	1	
PET			\		\	\						\				3	1	
Partial																		
OFT-M		\														1	0	
OFT-V		\								\						1	1	
OFT-P							\	\	\				\	\		5	0	
TDI					\					\					\			3

Moment	31	32	33	34	35*	36	37	38	39	40*	41	42	43	44	45*	S	P	T
AET		\			\											1	1	
PET	\		\	\							\	\	\	\		7	0	
Partial																		
OFT-M								\	\						\	2	1	
OFT-V						\	\									2	0	
OFT-P										\						0	1	
TDI										\					\			2

Moment	46	47	48	49	50*	51	52	53	54	55*	56	57	58	59	60*	S	P	T
AET					\											0	1	
PET		\	\	\						\					\	3	2	
Partial																		
OFT-M											\					1	0	
OFT-V											\	\				2	0	
OFT-P						\	\	\	\					\		5	0	
TDI															\			1

		Target Student			*Peer Comparison			Teacher	
	S AET	9	% AET	18.8	S AET	5	% AET	41.7	S TDI	7
Total	S PET	18	% PET	37.5	S PET	4	% PET	33.3	% TDI	58.3
Intervals	S OFT-M	6	% OFT-M	12.5	S OFT-M	2	% OFT-M	16.7	
Observed	S OFT-V	8	% OFT-V	16.7	S OFT-V	2	% OFT-V	16.7	Total Intervals
48	OFT-P	13	% OFT-P	27.1	S OFT-P	2	% OFT-P	16.7	Observed	12

FIGURE 5. Completed Boss observation on Justin.

BOSS RESULTS

Student: Justin

Observer: JGL   Grade: 3

Date: 09/15/2009   Time: 9:51:27 A.M.   Task: Math

Setting: SmGp:TpSnt   Duration: 15 minutes   Interval: 15 seconds

Behavior	Target Student		Peer Student		Teacher	
	Count	Percent	Count	Percent	Count	Percent
AET	9	18.8%	5	41.7%	–	–
PET	18	37.5%	4	33.3%	–	–
OFT-M	6	12.5%	2	16.7%	–	–
OFT-V	8	16.7%	2	16.7%	–	–
OFT-P	13	27.1%	2	16.7%	–	–
TDI	–	–	–	–	7	58.3%
	Target Ints	48			Peer/Teacher Ints	12

	AET	PET	OFT-M	OFT-V	OFT-P	TDI
1	1	0	1	0	1	–
2	0	1	0	0	0	–
3	1	0	0	0	0	–
4	0	0	0	0	1	–
5	*1*	*0*	*0*	*0*	*1*	*0*
6	1	0	0	1	0	–
7	1	0	0	1	0	–
8	0	1	0	0	0	–
9	0	1	1	0	0	–
10	*1*	*0*	*0*	*1*	*0*	*0*
11	0	1	0	1	0	–
12	1	0	0	0	0	–
13	0	0	0	0	1	–
14	0	1	0	0	0	–
15	*0*	*1*	*1*	*0*	*0*	*1*
16	1	0	0	0	0	–
17	0	0	1	1	0	–
18	0	1	0	0	0	–
19	1	0	0	0	0	–
20	*0*	*1*	*0*	*0*	*0*	*1*
21	0	1	0	0	0	–
22	0	0	0	0	1	–
23	0	0	0	0	1	–
24	0	0	0	0	1	–
25	*0*	*0*	*0*	*1*	*0*	*1*
26	1	0	0	0	0	–
27	0	1	0	0	0	–
28	0	0	0	0	1	–
29	0	0	0	0	1	–
30	*1*	*0*	*0*	*0*	*0*	*1*

(cont.)

FIGURE 6. Report generated from the BOSS software for Justin. Note that italics indicate peer comparison observation.

	AET	PET	OFT-M	OFT-V	OFT-P	TDI
31	0	1	0	0	0	–
32	1	0	0	0	0	–
33	0	1	0	0	0	–
34	0	1	0	0	0	–
35	1	0	*0*	*0*	*0*	*0*
36	0	0	0	1	0	–
37	0	0	0	1	0	–
38	0	0	1	0	0	–
39	0	0	1	0	0	–
40	*0*	*0*	*0*	*0*	*1*	*1*
41	0	1	0	0	0	–
42	0	1	0	0	0	–
43	0	1	0	0	0	–
44	0	1	0	0	0	–
45	*0*	*0*	*1*	*0*	*0*	*1*
46	0	0	0	0	0	–
47	0	1	0	0	0	–
48	0	1	0	0	0	–
49	0	1	0	0	0	–
50	*1*	*0*	*0*	*0*	*0*	*0*
51	0	0	0	0	1	–
52	0	0	0	0	1	–
53	0	0	0	0	1	–
54	0	0	0	0	1	–
55	*0*	*1*	*0*	*0*	*0*	*0*
56	0	0	1	1	0	–
57	0	0	0	1	0	–
58	0	0	0	0	0	–
59	0	0	0	0	1	–
60	*0*	*1*	*0*	*0*	*0*	*1*

Behavior Legend

AET	Actively Engaged in Task
PET	Passively Engaged in Task
OFT-M	Off-Task Motor
OFT-V	Off-Task Verbal
OFT-P	Off-Task Passive
TDI	Teacher-Directed Instruction

FIGURE 6. *(cont.)*

In the example shown in Figure 5, the target student was observed for a total of 48 intervals, peers for 12 intervals. Across the observation, AET for the target student was observed nine times, resulting in 18.8% of the intervals. For the peer comparison students, AET was observed five times out of 12 intervals, or 41.7% of the intervals. Calculations for all categories should result in the summary on the bottom of Figure 5.

If an observer is using the BOSS software, all of these calculations are automatically provided at the end of the observation and displayed on the PDA. The data are automatically stored and transferred to a personal computer through the HotSync process. A report is then generated based on the observation (see Figure 6).

Moment	1	2	3	4	5*	6	7	8	9	10*	11	12	13	14	15*	S	P	T
AET	\		\		\	\	\			\		\				5	1	
PET		\						\	\		\			\	\	5	2	
Partial																		
OFT-M	\								\						\	2	0	
OFT-V						\	\			\	\					3	0	
OFT-P	\			\	\								\			3	0	
TDI					\										\			1

FIGURE 7. First 15 intervals of BOSS observation for Justin. *, peer comparison.

Moment	1	2	3	4	5*	6	7	8	9	10*	11	12	13	14	15*	S	P	T
AET	\		\		\	\	\			\		\				5	2	
PET		\						\	\		\			\	\	5	1	
Partial																		
OFT-M	\								\						\	2	1	
OFT-V						\	\			\	\					3	1	
OFT-P	\			\	\								\			3	1	
TDI					\										\			1

FIGURE 8. First 15 intervals of BOSS observation for Justin, scored for peer comparison students. *, peer comparison.

Moment	1	2	3	4	5*	6	7	8	9	10*	11	12	13	14	15*	S	P	T
AET	\		\		\	\	\			\		\				5	2	
PET		\						\	\		\			\	\	5	1	
Partial																		
OFT-M	\								\						\	2	1	
OFT-V						\	\			\	\					3	1	
OFT-P	\			\	\								\			3	1	
TDI					\										\			2

FIGURE 9. First 15 intervals of BOSS observation for Justin, scored for TDI. *, peer comparison.

INTERPRETATION OF BOSS DATA

Interpretation of the BOSS data can involve analysis of several aspects of classroom behavior. First, the BOSS shows the levels of academic engagement and nonengagement for the targeted student in the particular setting of observation. By comparing the combined percentages of AET and PET against those of the three OFT categories, the observer can establish the amount of a student's on- and off-task behavior. These data can provide the observer with information about the extent to which the target student is effectively engaged in the learning process.

Second, observations across multiple settings make it possible to determine relative differences in the target student's academic engagement in different instructional environments. For example, it may be found that a student has much higher levels of on-task behavior when he/she is in a teacher-led setting than when involved in independent seatwork.

Third, by examining the relative differences between AET and PET, the observer can determine whether the opportunities to respond (AET level) for a student are of a sufficient number to provide clear evidence of academic progress. Students who are struggling in school are often found to have relatively low levels of AET even when they are on-task.

Fourth, and most importantly, the observer can compare the performance of the target student against the student's peers. Use of this type of local normative data is crucial in understanding the degree to which the levels of behavior obtained for the target student differ from the expected performance of the student's classmates. At times, a student who appears to have very low levels of on-task behavior may be found to have a level equivalent to those of his/her peers, suggesting that the student's behavior may not be beyond the expectations set by the classroom teacher. On the other hand, a student appearing to have very high levels of on-task behavioral performance may be viewed as not meeting classroom expectations. When comparisons are made to the student's peers, it may become evident that although the student's level is high, it is significantly lower than the levels of his/her peers.

One of the most frequently asked questions related to conducting systematic observation is, "How much observation is needed?" The answer is, "It depends." Accurate observations require at least 10–15 minutes. Optimally, observations should be 20–30 minutes each. In the best of all possible worlds, the observation should be repeated over 2–3 days, and possibly across different types of academic settings (e.g., independent work in reading, small-group activities in math, large-group activities in science). Obviously, the practical restrictions of time may limit how much observation can be done. So the question is whether a single observation can be enough.

The key to good observation is that it accurately represents the child's behavior at the time of the observation and at other times of the day. If a child's behavior tends to be highly variable from day to day or hour to hour, a single observation at one time in one setting may not be sufficient. Likewise, if a child's behavior changes because there is an observer in the classroom, or the child is having a "good day," a single observation may not be enough. Certainly, some degree of stable responding from day to day is important; however, the problem of some children is precisely that they are inconsistent, so expecting consistency in those cases is unrealistic.

One way to address this problem is always to ask the teacher whether the behavior seen that day was typical of the student's performance. If it was, then the one observation may be enough. However, if the child's behavior was atypical of what the teacher thinks is his/her usual behavior, than additional observation is needed.

Another important issue to consider in deciding whether enough observation has been done is whether the situation in which the behavior was observed represents where the problems tend to occur. For example, although the teacher notes that Josh has problems during independent seatwork activities, an important question for the teacher is whether there are equal problems in math and reading. One hypothesis about Josh's behavior may be that his skill levels differ across subject matter, and the differential skill levels result in differential behavioral outcomes. Thus, it may be crucial to conduct observations during independent seatwork periods in both a math and reading activities.

The rule of thumb often recommended is that observers should plan to conduct at least three observations. If behavior is consistent across two observations, than the third can perhaps be bypassed. If the behavior is not consistent after three observations, than at least one additional observation should be conducted. It is important to note that the decision about when sufficient observation has been conducted must be a clinical decision made from sound clinical judgment. There is no single rule that can be applied in all cases.

In the example shown in Figure 5, the student Justin was observed during his math class. Throughout the observation, the teacher was engaged in teaching a small group (six students) in which Justin was included. Peer comparison data for this observation were collected among the other five students in Justin's small group. The observation lasted for 15 minutes and was conducted at 10:30 A.M. Justin's overall level of on-task behavior is much lower than that of his peers. In total, Justin was academically engaged for 56.3% of the observed intervals, whereas his peers remained engaged for 75.0% of the observed intervals. In addition, when Justin was engaged, he spent the largest proportion of his time (37.5% of the intervals) in passive rather than active forms of engagement. In contrast, his peers were actively engaged for 41.7% of the intervals.

When Justin was off-task, he was primarily nonengaged in passive ways. Typically, this involved looking away from his work and staring out the windows but also included his getting out of his seat and speaking to his peers. However, these off-task behaviors by Justin were comparable to those of his classmates.

Justin's teacher was engaged in directed teaching activities for approximately 58.3% of the observed intervals. During intervals when Justin's teacher was not instructing the class, she was observed in classroom management activities, such as redirecting Justin and other students to pay attention to her direction.

In regard to interpreting data from the BOSS, it is important to note that the observer does not view the level of behavior obtained through the observation to represent an estimate of the amount of time that a behavior would occur. Because the observation system is derived from a time-sampling strategy, it would be inaccurate to say that the behavior occurred for ____% of the time. This is especially true since partial-interval recording systems (such as those used here for the off-task behaviors and TDI) are likely to overestimate the actual rate of a behavior's occurrence. It is also important to note that the data collected for the target student are likely to be more reliable and stable then the data collected for peer comparison purposes. The more observation intervals, the better the stability of the measure. In this observation example, there were 48 observations of the target student and only 12 of the peers. Data collected on peers must be considered cautiously in the interpretation of results.

BEHAVIORAL OBSERVATION OF STUDENTS IN SCHOOLS (BOSS)

Child Observed: _____   Academic Subject: _____

Date: _____   Setting: _____ ISW:TPsnt _____ SmGp:TPsnt

Observer: _____   _____ ISW:TSmGp _____ LgGp:TPsnt

Time of Observation: _____   Interval Length: _____   Other: _____

Moment	1	2	3	4	5*	6	7	8	9	10*	11	12	13	14	15*	S	P	T
AET																		
PET																		
Partial																		
OFT-M																		
OFT-V																		
OFT-P																		
TDI																		

Moment	16	17	18	19	20*	21	22	23	24	25*	26	27	28	29	30*	S	P	T
AET																		
PET																		
Partial																		
OFT-M																		
OFT-V																		
OFT-P																		
TDI																		

Moment	31	32	33	34	35*	36	37	38	39	40*	41	42	43	44	45*	S	P	T
AET																		
PET																		
Partial																		
OFT-M																		
OFT-V																		
OFT-P																		
TDI																		

Moment	46	47	48	49	50*	51	52	53	54	55*	56	57	58	59	60*	S	P	T
AET																		
PET																		
Partial																		
OFT-M																		
OFT-V																		
OFT-P																		
TDI																		

	Target Student			*Peer Comparison			Teacher	
Total Intervals Observed	S AET _____	% AET _____	S AET _____	% AET _____	S TDI _____
	S PET _____	% PET _____	S PET _____	% PET _____	% TDI _____
	S OFT-M _____	% OFT-M _____	S OFT-M _____	% OFT-M _____	Total Intervals Observed _____
	S OFT-V _____	% OFT-V _____	S OFT-V _____	% OFT-V _____	
_____	OFT-P _____	% OFT-P _____	S OFT-P _____	% OFT-P _____	

(cont.)

BEHAVIORAL OBSERVATION OF STUDENTS IN SCHOOLS (BOSS)

Child Observed: _____   Academic Subject: _____

Date: _____   Setting: _____ ISW:TPsnt   _____ SmGp:TPsnt

Observer: _____   _____ ISW:TSmGp   _____ LgGp:TPsnt

Time of Observation: _____   Interval Length: _____ Other: _____

Moment	61	62	63	64	65*	66	67	68	69	70*	71	72	73	74	75*	S	P	T
AET																		
PET																		
Partial																		
OFT-M																		
OFT-V																		
OFT-P																		
TDI																		

Moment	76	77	78	79	80*	81	82	83	84	85*	86	87	88	89	90*	S	P	T
AET																		
PET																		
Partial																		
OFT-M																		
OFT-V																		
OFT-P																		
TDI																		

Moment	91	92	93	94	95*	96	97	98	99	100*	101	102	103	104	105*	S	P	T
AET																		
PET																		
Partial																		
OFT-M																		
OFT-V																		
OFT-P																		
TDI																		

Moment	106	107	108	109	110*	111	112	113	114	115*	116	117	118	119	120*	S	P	T
AET																		
PET																		
Partial																		
OFT-M																		
OFT-V																		
OFT-P																		
TDI																		

	Target Student			*Peer Comparison			Teacher	
Total Intervals Observed	S AET ____	% AET ____		S AET ____	% AET ____		S TDI	____
	S PET ____	% PET ____		S PET ____	% PET ____		% TDI	____
	S OFT-M ____	% OFT-M ____		S OFT-M ____	% OFT-M ____		Total Intervals Observed	____
	S OFT-V ____	% OFT-V ____		S OFT-V ____	% OFT-V ____			
____	OFT-P ____	% OFT-P ____		S OFT-P ____	% OFT-P ____			

(cont.)

BEHAVIORAL OBSERVATION OF STUDENTS IN SCHOOLS (BOSS)

Child Observed: _____ Academic Subject: _____

Date: _____ Setting: _____ ISW:TPsnt _____ SmGp:TPsnt _____

Observer: _____ _____ ISW:TSmGp _____ LgGp:TPsnt _____

Time of Observation: _____ Interval Length: _____ Other: _____

Moment	121	122	123	124	125*	126	127	128	129	130*	131	132	133	134	135*	S	P	T
AET																		
PET																		
Partial																		
OFT-M																		
OFT-V																		
OFT-P																		
TDI																		

Moment	136	137	138	139	140*	141	142	143	144	145*	146	147	148	149	150*	S	P	T
AET																		
PET																		
Partial																		
OFT-M																		
OFT-V																		
OFT-P																		
TDI																		

Moment	151	152	153	154	155*	156	157	158	159	160*	161	162	163	164	165*	S	P	T
AET																		
PET																		
Partial																		
OFT-M																		
OFT-V																		
OFT-P																		
TDI																		

Moment	166	167	168	169	170*	171	172	173	174	175*	176	177	178	179	180*	S	P	T
AET																		
PET																		
Partial																		
OFT-M																		
OFT-V																		
OFT-P																		
TDI																		

	Target Student		*Peer Comparison		Teacher	
Total Intervals Observed	S AET _____	% AET _____	S AET _____	% AET _____	S TDI _____	
	S PET _____	% PET _____	S PET _____	% PET _____	% TDI _____	
	S OFT-M _____	% OFT-M _____	S OFT-M _____	% OFT-M _____	Total Intervals Observed _____	
	S OFT-V _____	% OFT-V _____	S OFT-V _____	% OFT-V _____		
_____	OFT-P _____	% OFT-P _____	S OFT-P _____	% OFT-P _____		

Assessing Instructional Placement

Reading

IN A DIRECT ASSESSMENT OF READING, the oral reading rate is typically the metric used to assess student progress. However, this metric is only one of several that can be used for conducting a curriculum-based assessment of reading. When the examiner is interested in using a metric that may be more sensitive to changes in comprehension skills, two measures that may have value are the use of a maze technique and an oral retell technique. A maze technique presents students with a reading passage in which certain words are eliminated and the task is to supply the missing words.

A maze measure for assessing reading comprehension is available from edcheckup (*www.edcheckup.com*), AIMSweb® (*www.aimsweb.com*), and DIBELS (*www. dibel.org*). Grade-level passages are available for grades 1–8. Beginning with the second sentence, every seventh word is removed, with three choices available for the student. One of the words is correct, another is a closely related but incorrect response, and a third is a distracter. Students are asked to circle the correct word as they read the passage. They are given 3 minutes to read the passage, and the number of correct maze words per minute represents the score on the item. Figure 10 provides an example from the AIMSweb product of a paper-and-pencil version of the maze technique. Normative data from the aggregation of AIMSweb users are available to interpret the outcomes of student performance on the maze task.

The use of oral retell techniques may also be a valuable adjunct to a curriculum-based assessment of reading. In this technique, students are asked to read a passage and then retell what they read in their own words. The task can be done using silent and oral reading if the evaluator suspects that a student is having difficulties when asked to read aloud. The student's responses can be scored using a checklist or rating scale, such as that provided in Form 7 or 8.

Form 7 is used for narrative passages and provides an opportunity to examine whether students know the key elements of story grammar, such as story sense, setting, characters, key events, and resolution. This form can be used for almost any narrative passage.

Jason and Max picked next Friday to carry out their special mission. Friday was a week away. They **(agreed, had, branches)** so many things to accomplish. In **(plan, order, at)** to reach their final goal, the **(next, branches, boys)** made a plan for each day **(to, of, each)** the week. They had to work **(hard, creek, big)** every day to finish each task. **(Pile, Could, Had)** they do it all?

On Monday, **(creek, big, they)** agreed to meet and put plan **(near, wood, A)** into action. Plan A was to **(gather, work, day)** as many fallen branches as they **(could, on, had)** carry. They hauled the wood from **(neat, a, the)** edge of the cornfield and stacked **(agree, it, they)** in a big pile at the **(plan, edge, hauled)** of the forest.

On Tuesday, the **(rocks, by, boys)** met near the lazy creek and **(put, climb, wood)** plan B into motion. They dug **(up, near, the)** rocks the size of footballs from **(and, night, the)** creek's bottom. By dusk, they had **(rode, arranged, to)** the rocks in a neat circle **(a, next, up)** to the pile of branches they **(their, found, had)** hauled the night before.

On Wednesday, **(plan, the, work)** C was to climb into the **(attic, umbrellas, they)** above Jason's garage. They searched around **(Max, in, with)** flashlights and both found backpacks. They **(spoke, under, wore)** their packs as they rode their **(without, bikes, garage)** to the edge of the forest **(to, end, for)** complete the day's work.

On Thursday **(they, it, work)** rained. They had to drop the **(up, plan, forest)** for the day. Still, Jason and **(went, backpack, Max)** met at the end of their **(bikes, driveways, on)** under umbrellas. They quietly spoke. They **(rained, decided, tent)** their mission would work without plan **(D, fire, was)**.

When the sun went down on **(only, Friday, evening)**, they met at the edge of **(the, out, and)** forest. There sat their tent. They'd **(stacked, tasks, set)** it up on Wednesday evening. The **(circle, special, wood)** was ready to go into their **(campfire, many, night)** ring. Their next step was to **(big, build, climb)** a warm fire:

The mission to **(camp, step, the)** out was complete. The only tasks **(Max, now, next)** were to sit back and enjoy **(a, the, ring)** fruits of their labor.

Jason and Max picked next Friday to carry out their special mission. Friday was a week away. They **(had)** so many things to accomplish. In **(order)** to reach their final goal, the **(boys)** made a plan for each day **(of)** the week. They had to work **(hard)** every day to finish each task. **(Could)** they do it all?

On Monday, **(they)** agreed to meet and put plan **(A)** into action. Plan A was to **(gather)** as many fallen branches as they **(could)** carry. They hauled the wood from **(the)** edge of the cornfield and stacked **(it)** in a big pile at the **(edge)** of the forest.

On Tuesday, the **(boys)** met near the lazy creek and **(put)** plan B into motion. They dug **(up)** rocks the size of footballs from **(the)** creek's bottom. By dusk, they had **(arranged)** the rocks in a neat circle **(next)** to the pile of branches they **(had)** hauled the night before.

On Wednesday, **(plan)** C was to climb into the **(attic)** above Jason's garage. They searched around **(with)** flashlights and both found backpacks. They **(wore)** their packs as they rode their **(bikes)** to the edge of the forest **(to)** complete the day's work.

On Thursday **(it)** rained. They had to drop the **(plan)** for the day. Still, , Jason and **(Max)** met at the end of their **(driveways)** under umbrellas. They quietly spoke. They **(decided)** their mission would work without plan **(D)**.

When the sun went down on **(Friday)**, they met at the edge of **(the)** forest. There sat their tent. They'd **(set)** it up on Wednesday evening. The **(wood)** was ready to go into their **(campfire)** ring. Their next step was to **(build)** a warm fire.

The mission to **(camp)** out was complete. The only tasks **(now)** were to sit back and enjoy **(the)** fruits of their labor.

FIGURE 10. Example of maze task for grade 3 from AIMSweb. Copyright 2008 by NCS Pearson, INc. Reprinted by permission. All rights reserved.

Form 8 provides a similar scoring rubric for expository or informational passages. The broad categories for scoring this type of retell include examination of the main topic, primary supporting detail, and secondary supporting detail. Users of this form must examine passages that are used for retells and, prior to using the form, establish the primary and secondary supporting details for that specific passage.

ORAL RETELL TECHNIQUES

- **Step 1:** The examiner selects a passage for the student to read. The passage should be between 250 and 300 words for a student in grade 3 or above, or between 150 and 200 words for a student in grade 1 or 2. The passage used should also have a story or theme embedded in it.
- **Step 2:** The examiner asks the student to read the entire passage aloud and times the reading (first minute only) to determine the rate of words read correctly and incorrectly per minute.
- **Step 3:** The examiner then asks the student to retell the passage in his/her own words and records the response for later scoring. The retell should be done in the following sequence: If the student is able to complete the retell accurately, accordingly to Level A procedures, then Levels B, C, and D would not be done. The examiner should proceed to the next level of the retell technique if the student is unsuccessful at the preceding level.

  - Level A: *Nonprompted retell without passage.* The examiner asks the student to retell the story in the passage, without allowing him/her access to the passage. When the student cannot add anything else to his/her retell, he/she is stopped.
  - Level B: *Nonprompted retell with passage.* The examiner asks the student to retell the story in the passage, allowing him/her access to the passage. Again, when the student cannot add anything to the retell, he/she is stopped.
  - Level C: *Prompted retell without passage.* The examiner does not allow the student access to the passage but provides the student with a simple prompt about the passage. For example, in the first case example using a narrative passage, the evaluator might ask the student, "The main idea of this story was about a circus coming to town. Now tell me more about the story." The examiner can continue to prompt the student to see how many prompts are needed for the student to accurately recall the information read. The student is stopped when he/she cannot recall anything further. Similarly, in the second example where the student read an expository passage about flamingos, the evaluator might ask the student, "The main idea of this passage was interesting facts about flamingos. Tell me some things about flamingos you remember that make them special birds." The examiner can continue to prompt the student to see how many prompts are needed to provide supporting details to the main idea of the story.
  - Level D: *Prompted retell with access to passage.* The student is allowed to look at the passage as the examiner provides a simple prompt about the story.

For example, for the narrative story, the evaluator might say to the student, "The main idea of this story was about a circus coming to town. Now tell me more about the story." Similarly, for the expository story, the examiner might say, "The main idea of this passage was facts about flamingos. Tell me some of the interesting things about flamingos that you read in the passage." Again, the examiner can continue to prompt the student to see how many prompts are needed for the student to accurately recall the information read. The student is stopped when he/she cannot recall anything further.

• **Step 4:** The examiner scores the retell against the retelling scoring form provided or developed for the passage. Again, an example of such a scoring form is provided in Forms 7 and 8.

Another variation of the retell technique would ask the student to read the story silently to him/herself rather than aloud.

QUANTIFICATION OF RETELLING FOR NARRATIVE TEXT

Student's Name: _____

Book/Page: _____ Date: _____

Directions: Place a 1 next to each item the student includes in his/her retelling. Credit the gist, as well as the obvious recall. Place an * if you ask the child questions to aid recall.

			Level			
		A	B	C	D	
Story sense						
Theme:	Main idea or moral of story	☐	☐	☐	☐	(1)
Problem:	Difficulty to overcome	☐	☐	☐	☐	(1)
Goal:	What the character wants to happen	☐	☐	☐	☐	(1)
Title:	Name of the story (if possible)	☐	☐	☐	☐	(1)
Setting						
	When and where the story occurs	☐	☐	☐	☐	(1)
Characters						
	Name the main characters	☐	☐	☐	☐	(1)
Events/episodes						
	Initiating event	☐	☐	☐	☐	(1)
	Major events (climax)	☐	☐	☐	☐	(1)
	Sequence: retells in structural order	☐	☐	☐	☐	(1)
Resolution						
	Name problem solution for the goal	☐	☐	☐	☐	(.5)
	End of the story	☐	☐	☐	☐	(.5)

TOTAL ____ ____ ____ ____

QUANTIFICATION OF RETELLING FOR EXPOSITORY TEXT

Student's Name: _____

Title of Passage: _____ Date: _____

Instructions:

- Listen to the child's retell up to two times, while referring to the template provided.
- Circle **1** if the child included the item in his/her retell, and circle **0** if he/she omitted the item.
- For the "Topic" and "Main Idea" categories, circle **0** if he/she omitted the item or part of the item listed on the template, and circle **1** if he/she completely stated the item listed on the template.
- For "Primary Supporting Details" and "Secondary Supporting Details," circle **0** if he/she omitted the item, **1** if he/she provided **1** response, **2** if he/she provided **2** responses, **3** if he/she provided **3** responses, and **4** if he/she provided **4 or more** responses.
- Write the "Total Score" on the line provided (**0–10 points**).

Topic: • _____	**0 1**
Main idea: • _____	**0 1**
Primary supporting details: • _____ • _____ • _____ • _____ • _____ • _____ • _____ • _____	**0 1 2 3 4**
Secondary supporting details: • _____ • _____ • _____ • _____ • _____ • _____ • _____ • _____ • _____	**0 1 2 3 4**

TOTAL SCORE: _____

RETELL TECHNIQUES: EXAMPLES AND EXERCISES

Case Descriptions: Narrative Retell

Shawn was a fourth-grade student in a general education classroom. He was selected by his teacher as an average-performing student in the classroom. Troy was a fourth-grade student in the same general education classroom as Shawn. His teacher selected him as a student having significant problems in reading. Both students were asked to read the following passage and then to retell the story in their own words, without use of the passage (Level A retell). After reading each student's retell, readers are invited to complete the Quantification of Retelling for Narrative Text form provided for each one. A completed form is provided on the following page in each case.

Passage Read

The people of Lone Tree, Texas, often wonder why the circus never comes to their town. Almost nobody remembers the one time, years ago, that the circus did come to town.

Lone Tree was a busy cowtown. Two trains stopped there each day. On Saturday night folks from miles around came to town—ranchers, cowboys, Indians, and homesteaders. Bearpaw Smith's store had just about everything that the people needed. But there was one thing missing. None of these people had ever seen the circus.

Then one day a silent stranger came to Lone Tree and plastered the walls of Bearpaw Smith's store with circus posters. The circus was coming to town! The people were so excited, they could hardly wait for the day of the show. The big day finally arrived, and it would be a day to remember.

An hour before showtime the crowd on the midway and around the ticket wagon was already so great that it seemed impossible that the circus tent would be able to hold them all. And still the people came.

One of the latecomers was Clyde Jones, the mountain-lion hunter, with his pack of "lion hounds." The circus people said it was against the rules to take dogs into the tent. Clyde said his were the best hounds in the state and where he went they went. The ticket taker answered that this was one place they were not going to go. If Clyde wanted to see the circus, he'd have to leave his dogs outside. Clyde grumbled, but he did want to see the circus, so he tied the hounds to tent stakes and left them howling after him as he went inside.

Results of Retelling for Shawn

Rates: Words correct/minute = 131
Words incorrect/minute = 0

Verbatim transcript: "It's about a town in Texas, and they've never seen, like, a circus before, and they want to see it. And they know a store that has everything except for a circus. And one day the store gets plastered, and they find out there is going to be a circus coming, and when they see it they can't believe that everyone can all fit into the tent. And then there is a man that comes late and he has, like, hounds and he can't bring them in, so he just leaves them out. But he wanted to bring them in, but he had to leave them outside."

Instructions: On Exercise 1 (p. 67), score Shawn's retelling for Level A before looking at the scored form on page 68.

QUANTIFICATION OF RETELLING FOR NARRATIVE TEXT

Student's Name: _____

Book/Page: _____ Date: _____

Directions: Place a 1 next to each item the student includes in his/her retelling. Credit the gist, as well as the obvious recall. Place an * if you ask the child questions to aid recall.

			Level				
			A	B	C	D	
Story sense							
Theme:	Main idea or moral of story		☐	☐	☐	☐	(1)
Problem:	Difficulty to overcome		☐	☐	☐	☐	(1)
Goal:	What the character wants to happen		☐	☐	☐	☐	(1)
Title:	Name of the story (if possible)		☐	☐	☐	☐	(1)
Setting							
When and where the story occurs			☐	☐	☐	☐	(1)
Characters							
Name the main characters			☐	☐	☐	☐	(1)
Events/episodes							
Initiating event			☐	☐	☐	☐	(1)
Major events (climax)			☐	☐	☐	☐	(1)
Sequence: retells in structural order			☐	☐	☐	☐	(1)
Resolution							
Name problem solution for the goal			☐	☐	☐	☐	(.5)
End of the story			☐	☐	☐	☐	(.5)

TOTAL ____ ____ ____ ____

QUANTIFICATION OF RETELLING FOR NARRATIVE TEXT

Student's Name: Shawn

Book/Page: _____ Date: _____

Directions: Place a 1 next to each item the student includes in his/her retelling. Credit the gist, as well as the obvious recall. Place an * if you ask the child questions to aid recall.

		Level				
		A	B	C	D	
Story sense						
Theme:	Main idea or moral of story	☒	☐	☐	☐	(1)
Problem:	Difficulty to overcome	☒	☐	☐	☐	(1)
Goal:	What the character wants to happen	☒	☐	☐	☐	(1)
Title:	Name of the story (if possible)	☐	☐	☐	☐	(1)
Setting						
When and where the story occurs		☒	☐	☐	☐	(1)
Characters						
Name the main characters		☐	☐	☐	☐	(1)
Events/episodes						
Initiating event		☒	☐	☐	☐	(1)
Major events (climax)		☒	☐	☐	☐	(1)
Sequence: retells in structural order		☒	☐	☐	☐	(1)
Resolution						
Name problem solution for the goal		☒	☐	☐	☐	(.5)
End the story		☒	☐	☐	☐	(.5)

TOTAL   8   ___   ___   ___

Comment: Note that Shawn's performance at Level A suggests no need to move to other levels of the retell technique.

Results of Retelling for Troy

Rates: Words correct/minute = 55
Errors/minute = 3

Verbatim transcript: (*Long pause.*) "The people are saying there has never been a circus in town before. So one day they heard there was a circus coming to town. Everybody was so happy they couldn't wait for the day to come. (*Examiner: Anything else?*) No."

Instructions: On Exercise 2 (p. 70), score Troy's retelling for Level A before looking at the scored form on page 71.

QUANTIFICATION OF RETELLING FOR NARRATIVE TEXT

Student's Name: _____

Book/Page: _____ Date: _____

Directions: Place a 1 next to each item the student includes in his/her retelling. Credit the gist, as well as the obvious recall. Place an * if you ask the child questions to aid recall.

		Level				
		A	B	C	D	
Story sense						
Theme:	Main idea or moral of story	☐	☐	☐	☐	(1)
Problem:	Difficulty to overcome	☐	☐	☐	☐	(1)
Goal:	What the character wants to happen	☐	☐	☐	☐	(1)
Title:	Name of the story (if possible)	☐	☐	☐	☐	(1)
Setting						
When and where the story occurs		☐	☐	☐	☐	(1)
Characters						
Name the main characters		☐	☐	☐	☐	(1)
Events/episodes						
Initiating event		☐	☐	☐	☐	(1)
Major events (climax)		☐	☐	☐	☐	(1)
Sequence: retells in structural order		☐	☐	☐	☐	(1)
Resolution						
Name problem solution for the goal		☐	☐	☐	☐	(.5)
End of the story		☐	☐	☐	☐	(.5)

TOTAL ____ ____ ____ ____

QUANTIFICATION OF RETELLING FOR NARRATIVE TEXT

Student's Name: _Troy_

Book/Page: _____   Date: _____

Directions: Place a 1 next to each item the student includes in his/her retelling. Credit the gist, as well as the obvious recall. Place an * if you ask the child questions to aid recall.

			Level				
			A	B	C	D	
Story sense							
Theme:	Main idea or moral of story		☒	☐	☐	☐	(1)
Problem:	Difficulty to overcome		☐	☐	☐	☐	(1)
Goal:	What the character wants to happen		☐	☐	☐	☐	(1)
Title:	Name of the story (if possible)		☐	☐	☐	☐	(1)
Setting							
When and where the story occurs			☐	☐	☐	☐	(1)
Characters							
Name the main characters			☐	☐	☐	☐	(1)
Events/episodes							
Initiating event			☒	☐	☐	☐	(1)
Major events (climax)			☐	☐	☐	☐	(1)
Sequence: retells in structural order			☐	☐	☐	☐	(1)
Resolution							
Name problem solution for the goal			☐	☐	☐	☐	(.5)
End the story			☐	☐	☐	☐	(.5)

TOTAL   _2_   ___   ___   ___

Comment: Note that Shawn's performance at Level A suggests no need to move to other levels of the retell technique.

Case Descriptions: Expository Retell

Joseph was a fourth-grade student in a general education classroom. He was selected by his teacher as an average-performing student in her classroom. Nathan was a fourth-grade student in the same general education classroom as Joseph. His teacher selected him as a student having significant problems in reading in her class. Both students were asked to read the following passage and then to retell the story in their own words, without use of the passage (Level A retell). After reading each student's retell, readers are invited to complete the Quantification of Retelling for Expository Text form provided for each one (see Exercise 3 and Exercise 4). A completed form is provided on the following page in each case, with each student's correct responses denoted by shading.

Passage Read

Flamingos are large, pink-colored wading birds. Some may be five feet tall! They have very long, thin necks. They have very long, thin legs, too. They look as if they are walking on stilts. Their feet are webbed like a duck's feet. Flamingos can swim, and they can fly.

Flamingos are birds that live in the warm parts of the world. Some live in Florida in the United States. There are six different kinds of flamingos in the world. They live near salty lakes and rivers.

Flamingos are funny birds to watch. When a flamingo sleeps, it often stands on one leg. It tucks the other leg up under its wing. They often twist their necks around so they can lay their heads on their backs. Another funny thing about flamingos is their knees. Unlike our knees, flamingos' knees bend backwards.

Flamingos are good parents. They build nests in mud. The male and female build the nest together. They use their beaks to push mud into the shape of a volcano about twelve inches high. They also use small stones and feathers. It may take some pairs six weeks to make their nest!

They usually hatch only one egg at a time. Both the mother and father bird take turns sitting on the egg. When a flamingo baby gets hungry, it squawks. Both parents feed the baby. Flamingo parents feed babies a bright red liquid from their beaks. This liquid is called "crop milk." It is very high in fat and protein. It is produced by both the male and female birds in the upper digestive tract.

Flamingos live together in groups. A group of flamingos is called a *flock* or *colony*. Sometimes they live in colonies of over a million birds.

Results of Retelling for Joseph

Rates: Words correct/minute = 99
Words incorrect/minute = 2

Verbatim transcript: "Umm, they tell you what color they are that, umm, they're how tall they are—they're 5 feet . . . umm . . . that they have very long necks like–like a giraffe but it's kind of short a little . . . umm they have very thin legs also . . . Umm . . . that they live in mud habitats with their babies, and the male and the female take turns sitting on the fla—umm—ah, on the baby flamingo like in its egg . . . umm . . . when the flamingo baby gets hungry it, like, squawks or something, and it like gives like a signal. Flamingos can swim and they can fly . . . umm . . . when they sleep they turn their necks all around, lay them on their back, and they lay on one leg, and they, umm, don't hatch all at one time. They hatch one at a time, and they live together in groups called a *flock* or a *colony*, and they live in the warm parts of the world like Florida or the United States . . . umm . . . there are six different kinds of flamingos in the world. They live near salty lakes and rivers."

Instructions: On Exercise 3 (p. 74), score Joseph's retelling before looking at the scoring form on page 75.

QUANTIFICATION OF RETELLING FOR EXPOSITORY TEXT

Student's Name: _Jospeh_

Title of Passage: _Flamingos_   Date: _____

Instructions:

- Listen to the child's retell up to two times, while referring to the template provided.
- Circle **1** if the child included the item in his/her retell, and circle **0** if he/she omitted the item.
- For the "Topic" and "Main Idea" categories, circle **0** if he/she omitted the item or part of the item listed on the template, and circle **1** if he/she completely stated the item listed on the template.
- For "Primary Supporting Details" and "Secondary Supporting Details," circle **0** if he/she omitted the item, **1** if he/she provided **1** response, **2** if he/she provided **2** responses, **3** if he/she provided **3** responses, and **4** if he/she provided **4 or more** responses.
- Write the "Total Score" on the line provided (**0–10 points**).

Topic: • Flamingos	0 1
Main idea: • Interesting facts/information about flamingos or flamingos are birds	0 1
Primary supporting details: • Flamingos are large, pink-colored wading birds. • They live in the warm parts of the world. • They usually hatch only one egg at a time. • Both the mother and father bird take turns sitting on the egg. • Both parents make the nest. • Both parents feed the baby. • Flamingo parents feed babies a bright red liquid from their beaks. • Flamingos live together in groups/a group of flamingos is called a _flock_ or _colony_. • Flamingos can swim, and they can fly.	0 1 2 3 4
Secondary supporting details: • Some may be 5 feet tall. • They have very long, thin necks. • They have very long, thin legs/they look like they are walking on stilts. • Their feet are webbed like a duck's feet. • Some live in Florida in the United States. • They live near salty lakes and rivers. • When a flamingo sleeps, it often stands on one leg. It tucks the other leg up. • They often twist their necks around so they can lay their heads on their backs. • Flamingos' knees bend backwards. • Flamingo parents use their beaks to push mud into the shape of a volcano about 12 inches high/they also use small stones and feathers. • When a flamingo baby gets hungry, it squawks. • "Crop milk" is very high in fat and protein. • Sometimes they live in colonies of over a million birds.	0 1 2 3 4

TOTAL SCORE: _____

QUANTIFICATION OF RETELLING FOR EXPOSITORY TEXT

Student's Name: Jospeh

Title of Passage: Flamingos   Date:

Instructions:

- Listen to the child's retell up to two times, while referring to the template provided.
- Circle **1** if the child included the item in his/her retell, and circle **0** if he/she omitted the item.
- For the "Topic" and "Main Idea" categories, circle **0** if he/she omitted the item or part of the item listed on the template, and circle **1** if he/she completely stated the item listed on the template.
- For "Primary Supporting Details" and "Secondary Supporting Details," circle **0** if he/she omitted the item, **1** if he/she provided **1** response, **2** if he/she provided **2** responses, **3** if he/she provided **3** responses, and **4** if he/she provided **4 or more** responses.
- Write the "Total Score" on the line provided (**0–10 points**).

Topic: • Flamingos	0 (1)
Main idea: • Interesting facts/information about flamingos or flamingos are birds	(0) 1
Primary supporting details: • Flamingos are large, pink-colored wading birds. • They live in the warm parts of the world. • They usually hatch only one egg at a time. • Both the mother and father bird take turns sitting on the egg. • Both parents make the nest. • Both parents feed the baby. • Flamingo parents feed babies a bright red liquid from their beaks. • Flamingos live together in groups/a group of flamingos is called a *flock* or *colony*. • Flamingos can swim, and they can fly.	0 1 2 3 (4)
Secondary supporting details: • Some may be 5 feet tall. • They have very long, thin necks. • They have very long, thin legs/they look like they are walking on stilts. • Their feet are webbed like a duck's feet. • Some live in Florida in the United States. • They live near salty lakes and rivers. • When a flamingo sleeps, it often stands on one leg. It tucks the other leg up. • They often twist their necks around so they can lay their heads on their backs. • Flamingos' knees bend backwards. • Flamingo parents use their beaks to push mud into the shape of a volcano about 12 inches high/they also use small stones and feathers. • When a flamingo baby gets hungry, it squawks. • "Crop milk" is very high in fat and protein. • Sometimes they live in colonies of over a million birds.	0 1 2 3 (4)

TOTAL SCORE: 9

Results of Retelling for Nathan

Rates: Words correct/minute = 34
            Words incorrect/minute = 3

Verbatim transcript: "About flaming—it was about flaming—flaming—flaming—flamingos and about funny things that they can do and they're pink-colored one—one—one—one—one . . . umm . . . they build nets in mud the male and female build the nets together. They use their beaks."

Instructions: On Exercise 4 (p. 77), score Nathan's retelling before looking a the scoring from page 78.

Exercise 4: Blank Form for Nathan

QUANTIFICATION OF RETELLING FOR EXPOSITORY TEXT

Student's Name: Nathan

Title of Passage: Flamingos   Date:

Instructions:

- Listen to the child's retell up to two times, while referring to the template provided.
- Circle **1** if the child included the item in his/her retell, and circle **0** if he/she omitted the item.
- For the "Topic" and "Main Idea" categories, circle **0** if he/she omitted the item or part of the item listed on the template, and circle **1** if he/she completely stated the item listed on the template.
- For "Primary Supporting Details" and "Secondary Supporting Details," circle **0** if he/she omitted the item, **1** if he/she provided **1** response, **2** if he/she provided **2** responses, **3** if he/she provided **3** responses, and **4** if he/she provided **4 or more** responses.
- Write the "Total Score" on the line provided (**0–10 points**).

Topic: • Flamingos	0 1
Main idea: • Interesting facts/information about flamingos or flamingos are birds	0 1
Primary supporting details: • Flamingos are large, pink-colored wading birds. • They live in the warm parts of the world. • They usually hatch only one egg at a time. • Both the mother and father bird take turns sitting on the egg. • Both parents make the nest. • Both parents feed the baby. • Flamingo parents feed babies a bright red liquid from their beaks. • Flamingos live together in groups/a group of flamingos is called a *flock* or *colony*. • Flamingos can swim, and they can fly.	0 1 2 3 4
Secondary supporting details: • Some may be 5 feet tall. • They have very long, thin necks. • They have very long, thin legs/they look like they are walking on stilts. • Their feet are webbed like a duck's feet. • Some live in Florida in the United States. • They live near salty lakes and rivers. • When a flamingo sleeps, it often stands on one leg. It tucks the other leg up. • They often twist their necks around so they can lay their heads on their backs. • Flamingos' knees bend backwards. • Flamingo parents use their beaks to push mud into the shape of a volcano about 12 inches high/they also use small stones and feathers. • When a flamingo baby gets hungry, it squawks. • "Crop milk" is very high in fat and protein. • Sometimes they live in colonies of over a million birds.	0 1 2 3 4

TOTAL SCORE: _____

QUANTIFICATION OF RETELLING FOR EXPOSITORY TEXT

Student's Name: Nathan

Title of Passage: Flamingos   Date:

Instructions:

- Listen to the child's retell up to two times, while referring to the template provided.
- Circle **1** if the child included the item in his/her retell, and circle **0** if he/she omitted the item.
- For the "Topic" and "Main Idea" categories, circle **0** if he/she omitted the item or part of the item listed on the template, and circle **1** if he/she completely stated the item listed on the template.
- For "Primary Supporting Details" and "Secondary Supporting Details," circle **0** if he/she omitted the item, **1** if he/she provided **1** response, **2** if he/she provided **2** responses, **3** if he/she provided **3** responses, and **4** if he/she provided **4 or more** responses.
- Write the "Total Score" on the line provided (**0–10 points**).

Topic: • Flamingos	0 ①
Main idea: • Interesting facts/information about flamingos or flamingos are birds	0 1
Primary supporting details: • Flamingos are large, pink-colored wading birds. • They live in the warm parts of the world. • They usually hatch only one egg at a time. • Both the mother and father bird take turns sitting on the egg. • Both parents make the nest. • Both parents feed the baby. • Flamingo parents feed babies a bright red liquid from their beaks. • Flamingos live together in groups/a group of flamingos is called a *flock* or *colony*. • Flamingos can swim, and they can fly.	0 1 ② 3 4
Secondary supporting details: • Some may be 5 feet tall. • They have very long, thin necks. • They have very long, thin legs/they look like they are walking on stilts. • Their feet are webbed like a duck's feet. • Some live in Florida in the United States. • They live near salty lakes and rivers. • When a flamingo sleeps, it often stands on one leg. It tucks the other leg up. • They often twist their necks around so they can lay their heads on their backs. • Flamingos' knees bend backwards. • Flamingo parents use their beaks to push mud into the shape of a volcano about 12 inches high/they also use small stones and feathers. • When a flamingo baby gets hungry, it squawks. • "Crop milk" is very high in fat and protein. • Sometimes they live in colonies of over a million birds.	0 ① 2 3 4

TOTAL SCORE: 4

Math

ONE OF THE KEY ASPECTS OF CURRICULUM-BASED ASSESSMENT OF MATH is using "digits correct per minute" or "total digits" as a metric in the scoring of student performance. In addition, in order to develop more effective interventions, examiners need to be able to conduct an analysis of the types of errors students are making as they complete the math probes. This section of the workbook provides descriptions of how to score math probes using digits correct per minute, along with examples of conducting an analysis of errors. Practice exercises for both scoring and interpretation of math probes are included.

A second component to curriculum-based assessment of math is the evaluation of student performance on measures of mathematical concepts–applications. Scoring these types of measures is not complex; however, developing these types of measures can be quite time-consuming. An example of this type of measure, along with its scoring, is provided, with indications where readers can obtain commercial measures of mathematics concepts–applications.

USING DIGITS CORRECT IN SCORING MATH PROBES

Typically, when a student is asked to complete math problems, the teacher marks the student's response as either correct or incorrect. Even small and minor errors in the computation process result in the student's obtaining an incorrect answer. In assessing the outcomes of an instructional process, an examiner needs to use a metric that can be sensitive across time to the student's gradual acquisition of the skills required to complete computations accurately. Using the metric of *digits correct* rather than *problems correct* accomplishes this goal.

For example, a student asked to add two three-digit numbers may initially get 0 digits correct:

(1)
$$
\begin{array}{r}
356 \\
+\,678 \\
\hline
922
\end{array}
$$

Recognizing the student's lack of knowledge of regrouping principles, the teacher begins to teach the student how to regroup from the 1's to the 10's column. After some instruction, the student now does the following when given a similar type of problem:

(2)
$$
\begin{array}{r}
467 \\
+\,589 \\
\hline
946
\end{array}
$$

In this problem the student has one digit correct. After additional instruction, the student produces the results of problem (3):

(3)
$$
\begin{array}{r}
378 \\
+\,657 \\
\hline
1035
\end{array}
$$

The metric of digits correct makes evident the student's gradual acquisition of the regrouping concept. If the evaluator were to use only the problem's correctness or incorrectness to determine whether the student was learning the concept of regrouping, the student's gradual acquisition of the skill would not be evident—nor would the student receive the gradual reinforcement that encourages further effort.

SCORING DIGITS CORRECT
FOR ADDITION AND SUBTRACTION PROBLEMS

The calculation of digits correct when the student is completing addition or subtraction problems is fairly straightforward. Each correct digit <u>below</u> the answer line is counted. If the problem involves regrouping, and the student places numbers above the columns to indicate how much was carried to the next column, these numbers are not counted in the digits-correct figure.

Examples:

$$
\begin{array}{r}
12 \\
+\,4 \\
\hline
16
\end{array}
\text{ (2 digits correct)}
\qquad
\begin{array}{r}
145 \\
+\,672 \\
\hline
817
\end{array}
\text{ (3 digits correct)}
$$

$$
\begin{array}{r}
54 \\
-\,27 \\
\hline
27
\end{array}
\text{ (2 digits correct)}
\qquad
\begin{array}{r}
2675 \\
-\,1089 \\
\hline
1586
\end{array}
\text{ (4 digits correct)}
$$

In a math curriculum-based assessment, sets of problems are administered under timed conditions, and a calculation is made of the number of digits correct per minute. Exercise 5 provides an opportunity to practice scoring addition and subtraction math problems using digits correct per minute.

DIGITS CORRECT FOR ADDITION AND SUBTRACTION PROBLEMS

Addition and Subtraction Facts with Regrouping to 10's Column

A	B	C	D	E
15 − 9 ⎯⎯ 6	4 − 0 ⎯⎯ 4	76 + 17 ⎯⎯ 81	12 − 8 ⎯⎯ 4	1 + 8 ⎯⎯ 9
F	**G**	**H**	**I**	**J**
8 + 3 ⎯⎯ 11	76 + 6 ⎯⎯ 82	80 − 4 ⎯⎯ 84	47 − 38 ⎯⎯ 11	10 − 5 ⎯⎯ 5
K	**L**	**M**	**N**	**O**
2 + 8 ⎯⎯ 10	0 + 6 ⎯⎯ 6	57 − 9 ⎯⎯ 52	431 − 31 ⎯⎯ 400	15 + 66 ⎯⎯ 81

Scoring: Write in the number of digits correct and incorrect for each problem.

Problem	Digits Correct	Digits Incorrect
A		
B		
C		
D		
E		
F		
G		
H		
I		
J		
K		
L		
M		
N		
O		

Answer Key to Exercise 5

Problem	Digits Correct	Digits Incorrect
A	1	0
B	1	0
C	0	2
D	1	0
E	1	0
F	2	0
G	2	0
H	0	2
I	0	2
J	1	0
K	2	0
L	1	0
M	0	2
N	3	0
O	2	0

Comments

The results of this math probe show several things. First, the digits-correct data place the student within the instructional level for students working within second-grade materials. However, the digits-incorrect results show that the student is making too many errors to be considered instructional. Therefore, the outcome of the probe would demonstrate that the student is in the frustrational level for second-grade material. A careful examination of the probe, however, shows specifically the type of skills that the student has yet to learn. The results show that the student knows basic addition and subtraction facts. However, whenever faced with a problem in which regrouping was required, the student instead subtracted the lower from higher number. The probe suggests that the student has not yet acquired the knowledge of how to regroup in subtraction. Interestingly, the results of problems G and O indicate that the difficulties in regrouping may be specific to subtraction.

MAKE UP YOUR OWN ADDITION AND SUBTRACTION PROBLEM
EXERCISE HERE

A	B	C	D	E
F	G	H	I	J
K	L	M	N	O

Scoring: Write in the number of digits correct and incorrect for each problem.

Problem	Digits Correct	Digits Incorrect
A		
B		
C		
D		
E		
F		
G		
H		
I		
J		
K		
L		
M		
N		
O		

SCORING DIGITS CORRECT
FOR MULTIPLICATION PROBLEMS

When multiplication is the skill assessed, counting digits correct can become more complicated. If the problem involves double-digit multiplication, then several digits are usually written below the answer line prior to reaching the final response. Because double-digit multiplication involves the operations of both multiplication and addition, a student could potentially make errors in two types of problems; that is, a student could multiply correctly but add incorrectly, thus getting the wrong answer. Likewise, a student could multiply incorrectly but add correctly, again reaching the wrong answer. If the student were to receive credit only for both multiplying *and* adding correctly, he/she would be penalized unduly for performing only one incorrect operation. Given that these metrics need to be sensitive to change over time, this would be inappropriate.

As a general rule of thumb, when the metric of digits correct is used in scoring multiplication, a student is given credit for the digit if the operation was performed correctly even if the answer itself is incorrect. For example, if a student asked to multiply a two-digit by two-digit problem did the following:

$$
\begin{array}{r}
75 \\
\times\, 26 \\
\hline
\mathbf{450} \\
\mathbf{150} \\
\hline
28\mathbf{50}
\end{array}
$$

the problem would be scored by counting all digits correct below the answer line. There are a total of nine digits correct (indicated in bold) and two incorrect. Seven of the correct digits are the numbers 450 and 150(0), the last 0 being a place holder, and two digits are correct in the final answer. Thus, this student multiplied correctly but added incorrectly. The score suggests that the difficulties were in the addition portion of the problem, since the majority of digits would be scored for multiplication rather than addition.

In contrast, another student performing the same problem may have done the following:

$$
\begin{array}{r}
75 \\
\times\, 26 \\
\hline
435 \\
285 \\
\hline
\mathbf{3415}
\end{array}
$$

This problem would be scored as having four digits correct (shown in bold): one digit (the 0 place holder) under the 1's column under the answer line, plus the three digits showing correct multiplication and addition. In this case, the student multiplied mostly incorrectly and added only partially correctly. Again, counting all digits except the placeholder incorrect would penalize the student unduly, when the real difficulty is only in multiplication—not in addition or in understanding the correct method for setting up a double-digit multiplication problem.

Exercise 6 is provided for the reader to practice scoring two- and three-digit multiplication problems.

DIGITS CORRECT
FOR TWO- AND THREE-DIGIT MULTIPLICATION PROBLEMS

A	B	C	D	E
11 × 13 13 11 ——— 123	83 × 48 644 127 ——— 1914	27 × 34 108 81 ——— 918	756 × 8 5648	113 × 59 1017 668 ——— 7697
F	**G**	**H**	**I**	**J**
550 × 66 3300 1216 ——— 15460	186 × 59 1676 4530 ——— 6106	536 × 91 536 4824 ——— 48776	710 × 92 1420 6390 ——— 65320	284 × 67 1988 1704 ——— 19028

Scoring: Write in the number of digits correct and incorrect for each problem.

Problem	Digits Correct	Digits Incorrect
A		
B		
C		
D		
E		
F		
G		
H		
I		
J		

Answer Key to Exercise 6:

Problem	Digits Correct	Digits Incorrect
A	7	1
B	7	4
C	9	0
D	2	2
E	10	2
F	10	4
G	7	5
H	13	0
I	14	0
J	14	0

Comments

The results of this probe show that the student, in general, understands the procedure for conducting two- and three-digit multiplication. Errors in place value or setup of the problems are not evident. However, the student does make the mistake in operations when the second digit is supposed to be multiplied. On problems B and F, for example, the student added instead of multiplied. On problem G, the student erred in place values, which resulted in many errors. Finally, it is important to remember to give the student credit for leaving a blank (zero placeholder) in the appropriate columns in most problems. It should also be noted that when the student multiplied incorrectly, he/she sometimes added correctly. Thus, credit is given for the student's completion of the operation correctly.

MAKE UP YOUR OWN MULTIPLICATION PROBLEM EXERCISE HERE

A	B	C	D	E
F	G	H	I	J

Scoring: Write in the number of digits correct and incorrect for each problem.

Problem	Digits Correct	Digits Incorrect
A		
B		
C		
D		
E		
F		
G		
H		
I		
J		
K		
L		
M		
N		
O		

SCORING DIGITS CORRECT FOR DIVISION PROBLEMS

Division creates several unique problems in the scoring of digits correct and incorrect. Division involving two or more digits requires that students perform three operations: division, multiplication, and subtraction. If one tries to use the digits correct and incorrect metric, it quickly becomes very complex to accurately score these problems. As with multiple-digit multiplication, the rule of thumb for scoring digits correct for division is that digits are counted as correct if the operation is performed correctly and the correct place value is used. For example, in the following example the student begins the long division problem correctly. (The student's work is shown on the left, the problem done entirely correctly is shown on the right.)

$$
\begin{array}{r}
\mathbf{283} \\
25\overline{)7375} \\
\mathbf{50} \\
\mathbf{237} \\
\mathbf{200} \\
75 \\
\underline{50} \\
\mathbf{25}
\end{array}
\qquad
\begin{array}{r}
296 \\
25\overline{)7375} \\
\underline{50} \\
237 \\
\underline{225} \\
125 \\
\underline{125} \\
0
\end{array}
$$

The student begins by dividing correctly (i.e., 73/25 = 2) and multiplies correctly (i.e., 2 × 25 = 50). He/she places the 50 under the correct columns and subtracts correctly (i.e., 73 − 50 = 23), and carries down the 7 from the next column. No errors have been made so far. He/she then makes an error in division (i.e., 237/25 = 8) but does multiply correctly (i.e., 25 × 8 = 200). He/she then makes an error in subtraction (i.e., 237 − 200 = 7) and carries down the 5 from the next column. He/she divides correctly but multiplies incorrectly (i.e., 25 × 3 = 50). Finally, he/she subtracts correctly. He/she is unsure what to do with the remainder, which, of course, is incorrect in the problem. In this problem, using the rule that correct operations are counted as correct digits, the student scores 14 digits correct (see the items in bold) and three incorrect. Looking at the type of errors provides clues as to the student's difficulties (in this case, he erred in basic division), but the scoring of the problem became complex, since many of the digits derived by the student did not match the correct solution to the problem. Furthermore, once the error in division was made, the remainder of the problem was incorrect.

A modification to the scoring procedure can reduce the problems that emerge in long division when using the rule of counting correct operations as correct. One simply compares the student's long division to a correct model of long division. The number of digits correct is summed and a percentage of correct digits out of the total digits possible for the problem is calculated.

The same example is presented below, with the student's work on the left and the model of the correct answer on the right. However, the scoring procedure used here is the percentage of correct digits. Only those digits that are in the correct place and with the correct value are counted.

```
        283                    296
   25)7375                25)7375
        50                     50
       237                    237
       200                    225
        75                    125
        50                    125
        25                      0
```

In the example, the student is given credit for the initial correct division (i.e., 73/25 = 2) and multiplication (i.e., 25 × 2 = 50). The student subtracted correctly (i.e., 73 – 50 = 23), brought the correct number down to the next column, but began to make errors when he/she divided incorrectly (i.e., 237/25 = 8). From this point forward, the only digits that were counted as correct were the 2 and 5, which were correct compared to the model. The total number of digits that was possible in the problem was 18 (17 digits plus a zero remainder; if a student did not write the zero, he/she would be given credit for an implied digit). This student had 8 of 18 digits correct, or 44.4% of the total possible digits correct. It is strongly suggested that this method of scoring long division be used.

Exercise 7 provides opportunities to practice scoring division problems for digits correct using the method of matching the student's performance against a correct model.

DIGITS CORRECT FOR DIVISION PROBLEMS
USING THE MATCH-TO-MODEL METHOD
(CORRECT DIGITS IN SAMPLE IN BOLDFACE)

A	B	C	D	E
50 R3 14)703 **70** 3	**1410** R2 3)452 **3** **15** 12 32 30 2	**10** R4 88)884 **88** **04** 0 4	**440** 22)9950 88 **1150** 880 70	**303** 29)8787 87 **8** **0** **87** **87** **0**
A—Correct Model	**B**—Correct Model	**C**—Correct Model	**D**—Correct Model	**E**—Correct Model
50 R3 14)703 70 *3 3 0 OR 3 *0 in this position is implicit and counted as a digit correct.	150 R2 3)452 3 15 15 *2 2 0 OR 2 *0 in this position is implicit and counted as a digit correct.	10 R4 88)884 88 *4 4 0 OR 4 *0 in this position is implicit and counted as a digit correct.	452 R6 22)9950 88 115 110 50 44 6	303 29)8787 87 *8 OR 87 0 87 87 0 87 0** *0 in this position is implicit and counted as a digit correct. **0 remainder is implicit and counted as a correct digit.

Answer Key to Exercise 7:

Problem	Actual Digits Correct	Possible Correct
A	8	8
B	5	12
C	8	8
D	6	16
E	13	13

Comments

Notice that when a remainder is present, the student is given credit for either indicating a remainder in the answer (e.g., writing "R2" in the answer) or leaving the remainder under the last subtraction. He/she is not given credit for both. The student is not given additional credit for remainders of 0. However, he/she is given credit for implied 0 digits. For example, in problem C, the student actually wrote in the 0 digit when subtracting 88 – 88. In problem A, the student did not actually write down the 0 when he/she subtracted 70 – 70; however, this digit was counted in the number of digits correct and possible for the problem. In addition, when student used appropriate shortcuts, he/she was credited for all digits to solve the problem, as if he/she had not used shortcuts. Examples A, B, C, and E illustrate the use of a shortcut and the full model for completing the problem.

MAKE UP YOUR OWN DIVISION PROBLEM EXERCISE HERE

A	B	C	D	E
F	G	H	I	J
K	L	M	N	O

Scoring: Write in the number of digits correct and incorrect for each problem.

Problem	Digits Correct	Digits Incorrect
A		
B		
C		
D		
E		
F		
G		
H		
I		
J		
K		
L		
M		
N		
O		

MATH CONCEPTS–APPLICATIONS

A curriculum-based assessment (CBA) of mathematics needs to go beyond math computation. Determining the ability of children to engage in problem solving, to apply mathematical principles to problems in geometry, time, money, measurement, graphing, numeration, and other such skills, is crucial to fully identifying targets for potential intervention. Assessing student performance across time in these skills provides strong opportunities for linking the assessment and instructional process.

Several commercial products are available to help evaluators conduct a CBA for math concepts–applications. For example, Schoolhouse Technologies (*www. schoolhousetech.com*) offers sets of worksheets that cover almost every area of mathematics. These worksheets contain single-skill problems that allow in-depth assessment of each area of math applications. Products available from *www.edhelper.com* and *aplusmath.com* allow users to build their own mixed-skills worksheet. AIMSweb® also has a set of concepts–applications probes available for purchase.

Another product that has been found to be very user friendly is available from Pro-Ed, Inc. (*www.proedinc.com*). Developed and revised by Fuchs, Hamlett, and Fuchs (1999) as part of a computerized progress monitoring system, this product contains 30 mixed-skills worksheets each for grades 2–8. The worksheets are scored by summing the number of correct answers that a student attains and dividing by the total number of possible correct problems. An example of one of these worksheets in provided in Figure 11.

Name _____ Date _____ Test 14 Page 2

Column C	Applications 3	Column D

(9)

Write <, >, or =
in each blank.

$\dfrac{2}{4}$ _____ $\dfrac{1}{2}$

$\dfrac{1}{4}$ _____ $\dfrac{3}{4}$

(10)

Write a number in each blank.

Of these numbers,

6582   7013   6569

_____ is the smallest.

_____ is the largest.

(11)

How much money?

_____

(12) Write the letter in the blank .

About how long is a hammer?

(A) 1 in.

(B) 1 ft

_____   (C) 1 mi

(13)

Third Graders Read Comic Books

Write a number in each blank.

How many more students read
Superman than Far Side?   _____

What is the total number of students
who read comic books?   _____

How many students read Batman?   _____

(14) Kimuli has 340 baseball cards and 72
comic books. On Monday he gave 36
baseball cards to his friends. How many
baseball cards does he have left?

_____

(15)   Rewrite

$4\overline{)20}^{\,5}$

as:

_____ ÷ _____ = _____

FIGURE 11. Example of a concepts–application probe for grade 3. From Fuchs, Hamlett, and Fuchs (1999). Copyright 1999 by Pro-Ed, Inc. Reprinted by permission.

Spelling

USING CORRECT LETTER SEQUENCES
IN SCORING SPELLING

As we have just seen, an examiner provides students with partial credit for responses in math using the digits correct metric rather than simply problems correct. An analogous metric exists for spelling: "correct letter sequences." By counting the number of correct consecutive letters rather than just the words spelled completely correctly, the examiner can detect small improvements in a student's responses. In addition, the types of errors made can be diagnostic; they can help the examiner identify the skills that a student has mastered and the ones that need to be targeted in future interventions.

Scoring correct letter sequences can be quite tedious and time-consuming. Fuchs, Fuchs, Hamlett, and Allinder (1991) used a computer program that provided the evaluator with automatic scoring for correct letter sequences. Although the program is no longer available, the output of the program offers an excellent examination of the potential for analyzing miscues in spelling. An example of this output is provided in Figures 12 and 13.

SCORING CORRECT LETTER SEQUENCES

• **Step 1:** The examiner places a blank before the first and last letter of each word to be scored. The blank is considered as a correct phantom character and is used to enable the initial and ending letters of words to be counted. For example:

_ s a m p l e _

```
-----------------------------------------------------------------------
 NAME: Charles Landrum          Spelling 4            Date: 4/10      Page 1
-----------------------------------------------------------------------


 Corrects      (100% LS)              14 word(s)
 Near Misses   (60-99%  LS)           19 word(s)
 Moderate Misses (10-59% LS)          16 word(s)
 Far Misses    (0-19% LS)              1 word(s)
```

Type	Correct	Possible	Pct	Type	Correct	Possible	Pct
Sing cons	48	50	96	Final vow	3	7	42
Blend	7	10	70	Double	3	4	75
FSLZ	0	0	100	c/s	0	1	0
Single vow	21	31	67	c/ck	0	2	0
Digraph	6	8	75	-le	4	7	57
Vowel + N	6	8	75	Ch/tch	2	2	100
Dual cons	13	25	52	-dge	0	1	0
Final e	1	5	52	Vowel team	4	12	33
igh/ign	0	0	100	Suffix	5	6	83
ild/old	0	0	100	tion/sion	0	1	0
a+l+cons	0	0	100	ance/ence	0	0	100
Vowel + R	9	14	64	sure/ture	0	0	100

KEY ERRORS

Dual cons	Final e	Final vow
learner—leaner	alone—alon	taste—tast
sample—samble	knife—knif	hero—hearow
chart—chard	rare—rar	lazy—lazz
mumble—mobble	cube—cub	unlucky—unluke
tractor—trater		
apart—apeot		

FIGURE 12. Example of skills analysis in spelling from Monitoring Basic Skills Progress. From Fuchs, Fuchs, Hamlett, and Allinder (1991, p. 56). Copyright 1991 by the National Association of School Psychologists. Reprinted by permission of the publisher. *www.nasponline.org.*

- **Step 2:** A linking symbol (⌒) is used to connect each letter to the next, beginning with the initial blank before the first letter. These should be placed alternately above and below consecutive letters.

$$\_⌒s\_a⌒m\_p⌒l\_e⌒\_$$

- **Step 3:** The examiner counts the number of letter sequences that are correct. The word *sample* above has a total of seven possible correct letter sequences.

Special Scoring Situations

Certain words create a need for special rules and conventions. In particular, the presence of double consonants can be confusing when using the letter sequences metric. If the student omits one of the consonants, credit is given only once. By comparing the student's spelling with the correct spelling, this can become evident. For example, the word

$$\_⌒b\_u⌒b\_b⌒l\_e⌒\_$$

contains a total of seven possible letter sequences. A student who spells the word as

$$\_⌒b\_u⌒b\_l⌒e\_$$

Corrects (100% LS)

100	March . . . . March			
100	death . . . . death			
100	sometimes . . . . . sometimes			
100	thankful . . . . thankful			
100	baker . . . . baker			
100	uncover . . . . uncover			
100	shy . . . . shy			
100	weakness . . . . . . weakness			
100	forgot . . . . forgot			
100	eyes . . . . eyes			
100	army . . . . army			
100	powerless . . . . . powerless			
100	wife . . . . wife			
100	mix . . . . mix			

Near Misses (60–99% LS)

77	shipment . . . . shapment	Single vow		
75	instead . . . . insted	Vowel team		
75	patches . . . . patces	Digraph		
75	moisten . . . . mosten	Vowel team		
75	quieter . . . . quieter	Vowel team		
75	learner . . . . learner	Dual cons		
75	trouble . . . . trubble	Vowel team		
71	sample . . . . sample	Dual cons		
71	listen . . . . lesten	Single vow		
66	badge . . . . bage	-dge		
66	taste . . . . tast	Final vow		
66	chart . . . . chard		Dual cons	
66	alone . . . . alon	Final e		
66	restless . . . . reasless	Blend		
66	knife . . . . knif	Final e		
60	hero . . . . hearow	Final vow	Vowel + R	
60	rare . . . . rar		Final e	
60	cube . . . . cub	Final e		
60	lazy . . . . lazz	Final vow		

Moderate Misses (20–59% LS)

57	tickle . . . . teakle	C/ck	Single vow	
57	french . . . . fanch	Vowel + N	Blend	
57	mumble . . . . mobble	Dual cons	Single vow	
50	unlucky . . . . unluke	Final vow	c/ck	
50	apart . . . . apeot	Vowel + R	Dual cons	
44	calendar . . . . . . calendar	Vowel + R	Vowel + N	Sing cons
42	mumble . . . . mommbe	-le	Single vow	
40	rail . . . . real	Vowel team		
37	station . . . . stanch	tion/sion		
28	sample . . . . scembe	-le	Dual cons	Single vow
25	certain . . . . chanteen	Vowel team	Vowel + R	c/s
20	limb . . . . lem	Dual cons	Single vow	
20	treatment . . . . . . tempemt	Suffix	Vowel team	Blend
20	limb . . . . learn	Dual cons	Single vow	

Far Misses (0–19% LS)

14	giggle . . . . gelly	-le	Double	Single vow

FIGURE 13. Example of page 2 of a CBM skills analysis in spelling. From Fuchs, Fuchs, Hamlett, and Allinder (1991, p. 57). Copyright 1991 by the National Association of School Psychologists. Reprinted by permission of the publisher. *www.nasponline.org.*

would be scored as having six letter sequences correct. The connection between and *b*, *b* and *u*, *u* and *b* is correct. The lack of the second *b* results in an incorrect sequence (no second *b*), but other sequences are correct.

Exercises 8 and 9, for practicing the scoring of spelling using correct letter sequences, are provided.

SCORING FOR LETTERS IN SEQUENCE FOR SPELLING

Instructions: Listed below are the actual way in which students spelled words on a weekly spelling test. The correct spelling is provided in the next column. Indicate the number of correct letter sequences for each word. The following page provides an answer sheet.

Word Spelled by Student	Correct Spelling	Letter Sequences Correct/Total Possible	Word Spelled Correctly?
rain	rain		
belong	belong		
botin	button		
lat	salt		
clock	clock		
smart	smart		
stap	step		
shep	sheep		
mint	minute		
above	above		
greup	group		
hunt	hut		
kesz	crazy		
jock	joke		
mire	mirror		
riad	drove		
nose	noise		

ANSWER SHEET FOR EXERCISE 8

Note: The first two words are scored as examples.

Word Spelled by Student	Correct Spelling	Letter Sequences Correct/Total Possible	Word Spelled Correctly?
_⌒r_a⌒i_n⌒_	rain	5/5	✓
_⌒b_e⌒l_o⌒n_g⌒_	belong	7/7	✓
botin	button	2/7	
slat	salt	2/5	
clock	clock	6/6	✓
smart	smart	6/6	✓
stap	step	3/5	
shep	sheep	4/6	
mint	minute	3/7	
above	above	6/6	✓
greup	group	4/6	
hunt	hut	3/4	
kesz	crazy	0/6	
jock	joke	2/5	
mire	mirror	3/7	
riad	drove	0/6	
nose	noise	4/6	

SCORING FOR LETTERS IN SEQUENCE FOR SPELLING

Instructions: Listed below are the actual way in which students spelled words on a weekly spelling test. The correct spelling is provided in the next column. Indicate the number of correct letter sequences for each word. The following page provides an answer sheet.

Word Spelled by Student	Correct Spelling	Letter Sequences Correct/Total Possible	Word Spelled Correctly?
scad	scold		
srey	sorry		
tow	tall		
hapin	happen		
fi	fourth		
alive	alive		
give	given		
dip	drop		
terth	teeth		
beer	bear		
beck	drink		
sotp	stop		
north	north		
jell	jail		
thre	flower		
leve	leave		
insiad	inside		

ANSWER SHEET FOR EXERCISE 9

Note: The first two words are scored as examples.

Word Spelled by Student	Correct Spelling	Letter Sequences Correct/Total Possible	Word Spelled Correctly?
⌒s⌣c a d⌒	scold	3/6	
⌒s r e y⌒	sorry	2/6	
tow	tall		
hapin	happen		
fi	fourth		
alive	alive		✓
give	given		
dip	drop		
terth	teeth		
beer	bear		
beck	drink		
sotp	stop		
north	north		✓
jell	jail		
thre	flower		
leve	leave		
insiad	inside		

Written Language

Written language assessments collected as part of the assessment of academic skills problems can be scored in multiple ways. Each of these metrics is used for a somewhat different purpose.

SCORING FOR WORDS WRITTEN

The simplest metric is to count the total number of words written. This metric is a strategy commonly used when the purpose of the assessment is progress monitoring. When an evaluator is using this metric, a word is counted if it is separated from other words in the written material. Words are counted regardless of whether they are spelled correctly or are phonetically recognizable. For example, a student given the story starter "When my video game started predicting the future, I knew I had to . . . " wrote the following during a 3-minute period: "got my mom to check it out I was ckerd it was hard to recat but my mom holped me then my brather came in to my room he helped me to but he left my room want down." Notice that many of the "words" are not recognizable, nor did they make sense in the context of the story as subsequently dictated by the student. The number of words written, however, would be scored as 39.

SCORING FOR WRITING MECHANICS

When the evaluator is interested more in short-term monitoring and the development of effective interventions, strengths and weaknesses in the mechanics of writing need to be assessed. This is most easily accomplished by developing a checklist that can be used repeatedly after each written language assessment is administered. Form 9 provides an example of a quality evaluation measure that one could use for assessing mechanics such as capitalization, punctuation, sentence construction, paragraph construction, and appearance of the written product. Exercise 10 provides a set of written responses from students to practice scoring using all three sets of measures.

ASSESSING QUALITY OF LONGER WRITING SAMPLES

The evaluator may also be interested in the overall quality of the student's writing. Overall quality can be assessed by using holistic scoring metrics for longer, more elaborate assignments given as part of the instructional process. These measures usually assign scores on a scale (such as 1–5), with the criteria for each score described. Examples of two types of these scoring devices are provided in Forms 10 and 11.

QUALITY EVALUATION MEASURE FOR WRITTEN PRODUCTS—
ELEMENTARY LEVEL

Student Name: _____

Date: _____

Grade: _____

Rating Scale:

 3 = Skill used consistently and accurately throughout written product (> 95% of time)

 2 = Skill used frequently and accurately throughout written product (50–94% of time)

 1 = Skill used infrequently or inaccurately (< 50% of the time)

 0 = No evidence of skill

Capitalization

First words in sentences are capitalized	0	1	2	3
Proper nouns are capitalized	0	1	2	3
Capitals are not used improperly	0	1	2	3

Punctuation

Punctuation occurs at the end of each sentence	0	1	2	3
End punctuation is correct	0	1	2	3

Sentence Construction

Absence of run-on sentences	0	1	2	3
Absence of sentence fragments	0	1	2	3
Absence of nonsensical sentences	0	1	2	3

Paragraph Construction

Each paragraph contains a topic sentence	N/A	0	1	2	3
Each sentence within a paragraph relates to the topic sentence	N/A	0	1	2	3

Appearance of Written Product

Words are legible	0	1	2	3
Spacing is appropriate between letters/words	0	1	2	3
Margins are appropriate	0	1	2	3
Written product is neat, with correct spelling	0	1	2	3

TOTAL SCORE ____

CRITERIA FOR HOLISTIC WRITING ASSESSMENT

① Highly flawed—Not competent

    Ideas poorly communicated

    Frequent usage errors (such as agreement, pronoun misuse, tense)

    Incorrect or erratic use of capitalization, punctuation, and spelling conventions

    Sentence fragments and run-ons; few complete sentences

    No concept of paragraph construction

② Unacceptable—Not competent

    Poor organization of ideas

    Frequent usage errors (such as agreement, pronoun misuse, tense)

    Inconsistent use of capitalization, punctuation, and spelling conventions

    Sentence fragments and run-ons; few complete sentences

    Poor topic sentence; flawed paragraph development

③ Minimally competent—Acceptable

    Ideas sufficiently organized and communicated

    Only occasional usage errors (such as agreement, pronoun misuse, tense)

    Minimal number of sentence errors (fragments or run-ons)

    Paragraphs have topic sentences, supporting ideas, and closing sentences

    Some attempt at paragraph transition

④ Competent—Clear mastery

    Ideas clearly communicated and of a fairly mature quality

    No usage errors

    Correct capitalization, punctuation, and spelling

    No fragments or run-ons

    Effective paragraph construction

Note: A paper that is illegible, off the point, or a nonresponse is scored 0.

Source: Division of Curriculum and Instruction, Department of Elementary and Secondary Education, Milwaukee, Wisconsin, Public Schools.

CRITERIA FOR ANALYTICAL SCORING

	1	2	3	4	5	
Organization	Little or nothing is written. The essay is disorganized, incoherent, and poorly developed. The essay does not stay on the topic.		The essay is not complete. It lacks an introduction, well-developed body, or conclusion. The coherence and sequence are attempted but not adequate.		The essay is well organized. It contains an introductory, supporting, and concluding paragraph. The essay is coherent, ordered logically, and fully developed.	×6
Sentence Structure	The student writes frequent run-ons or fragments.		The student makes occasional errors in sentence structure. Little variety in sentence length or structure exists.		The sentences are complete and varied in length and structure.	×5
Usage	The student makes frequent errors in word choice and agreement.		The student makes occasional errors in word choice or agreement.		The usage is correct. Word choice is appropriate.	×4
Mechanics	The student makes frequent errors in spelling, punctuation, and capitalization.		The student makes an occasional error in mechanics.		The spelling, capitalization, and punctuation are correct.	×4
Format	The format is sloppy. There are no margins or indentations. Handwriting is inconsistent.		The handwriting, margins, and indentations have occasional inconsistencies—no title or inappropriate title.		The format is correct. The title is appropriate. The handwriting, margins, and indentations are consistent.	×1

Source: Adams County School District #12, 11285 Highline Drive, Northglenn, Colorado 80203.

SCORING BRIEF WRITTEN LANGUAGE SAMPLES: EXAMPLES AND EXERCISES

Below are three written samples, collected as 3-minute story starters during a direct assessment of written expression. All students were in the fifth grade. In exercises 10, 11, and 12, readers can practice using the Quality Evaluation Measure for Written Products—Elementary Level to score the samples. A scored form follows each blank form (answers are underlined).

Starter and Writing Samples

Starter: "When my video game started predicting the future, I knew I had to . . ."

Student 1: Bryan

"got my mom to check it out I was ckerd it was hard to recat but my mom holped me then my brother came in to my room he helped my to but he left my room want down."

Student 2: Valesa

"Get it to put back on my other game and when the future came on my board I was very surprised because it was talking to me and I did not now wat it was talking about and it just kep on talking to me and when it said I was going to live in mars I said y must I live on mars he said because you have to and I said how comes."

Student 3: Cary

"run and get my camera. I ran into my room to find it, it was gone. I wanted to see what it would do if I turned it off. I put my hand on the power button, and I felt a stinging shock on my finger. I ran to get my mom. By the time she got there, it was too late."

QUALITY EVALUATION MEASURE FOR WRITTEN PRODUCTS—
ELEMENTARY LEVEL

Student Name: _____

Date: _____

Grade: _____

Rating Scale:

  3 = Skill used consistently and accurately throughout written product
        (> 95% of time)

  2 = Skill used frequently and accurately throughout written product
        (50–94% of time)

  1 = Skill used infrequently or inaccurately
        (< 50% of the time)

  0 = No evidence of skill

Capitalization

First words in sentences are capitalized		0	1	2	3
Proper nouns are capitalized		0	1	2	3
Capitals are not used improperly		0	1	2	3

Punctuation

Punctuation occurs at the end of each sentence		0	1	2	3
End punctuation is correct		0	1	2	3

Sentence Construction

Absence of run-on sentences		0	1	2	3
Absence of sentence fragments		0	1	2	3
Absence of nonsensical sentences		0	1	2	3

Paragraph Construction

Each paragraph contains a topic sentence	N/A	0	1	2	3
Each sentence within a paragraph relates to the topic sentence	N/A	0	1	2	3

Appearance of Written Product

Words are legible	N/A	0	1	2	3
Spacing is appropriate between letters/words	N/A	0	1	2	3
Margins are appropriate	N/A	0	1	2	3
Written product is neat, with correct spelling	N/A	0	1	2	3

TOTAL SCORE ____

QUALITY EVALUATION MEASURE FOR WRITTEN PRODUCTS—
ELEMENTARY LEVEL

Student Name: Bryan

Date: 4-21-10

Grade: 5

Rating Scale:

    3 =   Skill used consistently and accurately throughout written product
             (> 95% of time)

    2 =   Skill used frequently and accurately throughout written product
             (50–94% of time)

    1 =   Skill used infrequently or inaccurately
             (< 50% of the time)

    0 =   No evidence of skill

Capitalization

First words in sentences are capitalized	_0_	1	2	3
Proper nouns are capitalized	_0_	1	2	3
Capitals are not used improperly	_0_	1	2	3

Punctuation

Punctuation occurs at the end of each sentence	_0_	1	2	3
End punctuation is correct	_0_	1	2	3

Sentence Construction

Absence of run-on sentences	_0_	1	2	3
Absence of sentence fragments	0	_1_	2	3
Absence of nonsensical sentences	0	1	2	_3_

Paragraph Construction

Each paragraph contains a topic sentence	_N/A_	0	1	2	3
Each sentence within a paragraph relates to the topic sentence	_N/A_	0	1	2	3

Appearance of Written Product

Words are legible	_N/A_	0	1	2	3
Spacing is appropriate between letters/words	_N/A_	0	1	2	3
Margins are appropriate	_N/A_	0	1	2	3
Written product is neat, with correct spelling	_N/A_	0	1	2	3

TOTAL SCORE _4_

QUALITY EVALUATION MEASURE FOR WRITTEN PRODUCTS— ELEMENTARY LEVEL

Student Name: _____

Date: _____

Grade: _____

Rating Scale:

    3 =   Skill used consistently and accurately throughout written product (> 95% of time)

    2 =   Skill used frequently and accurately throughout written product (50–94% of time)

    1 =   Skill used infrequently or inaccurately (< 50% of the time)

    0 =   No evidence of skill

Capitalization

First words in sentences are capitalized	0	1	2	3
Proper nouns are capitalized	0	1	2	3
Capitals are not used improperly	0	1	2	3

Punctuation

Punctuation occurs at the end of each sentence	0	1	2	3
End punctuation is correct	0	1	2	3

Sentence Construction

Absence of run-on sentences	0	1	2	3
Absence of sentence fragments	0	1	2	3
Absence of nonsensical sentences	0	1	2	3

Paragraph Construction

Each paragraph contains a topic sentence	N/A	0	1	2	3
Each sentence within a paragraph relates to the topic sentence	N/A	0	1	2	3

Appearance of Written Product

Words are legible	N/A	0	1	2	3
Spacing is appropriate between letters/words	N/A	0	1	2	3
Margins are appropriate	N/A	0	1	2	3
Written product is neat, with correct spelling	N/A	0	1	2	3

TOTAL SCORE ____

Exercise 11: Scored Form for Valesa

QUALITY EVALUATION MEASURE FOR WRITTEN PRODUCTS—
ELEMENTARY LEVEL

Student Name: _Valesa_

Date: _4-21-10_

Grade: _5_

Rating Scale:

    3 =   Skill used consistently and accurately throughout written product (> 95% of time)

    2 =   Skill used frequently and accurately throughout written product (50–94% of time)

    1 =   Skill used infrequently or inaccurately (< 50% of the time)

    0 =   No evidence of skill

Capitalization

First words in sentences are capitalized	0	_1_	2	3
Proper nouns are capitalized	0	1	_2_	3
Capitals are not used improperly	0	1	2	_3_

Punctuation

Punctuation occurs at the end of each sentence	_0_	1	2	3
End punctuation is correct	_0_	1	2	3

Sentence Construction

Absence of run-on sentences	0	1	2	_3_
Absence of sentence fragments	0	1	2	_3_
Absence of nonsensical sentences	0	1	2	_3_

Paragraph Construction

Each paragraph contains a topic sentence	_N/A_	0	1	2	3
Each sentence within a paragraph relates to the topic sentence	_N/A_	0	1	2	3

Appearance of Written Product

Words are legible	_N/A_	0	1	2	3
Spacing is appropriate between letters/words	_N/A_	0	1	2	3
Margins are appropriate	_N/A_	0	1	2	3
Written product is neat, with correct spelling	_N/A_	0	1	2	3

TOTAL SCORE   _15_

QUALITY EVALUATION MEASURE FOR WRITTEN PRODUCTS—
ELEMENTARY LEVEL

Student Name: _____

Date: _____

Grade: _____

Rating Scale:

3 = Skill used consistently and accurately throughout written product (> 95% of time)

2 = Skill used frequently and accurately throughout written product (50–94% of time)

1 = Skill used infrequently or inaccurately (< 50% of the time)

0 = No evidence of skill

Capitalization

First words in sentences are capitalized	0	1	2	3
Proper nouns are capitalized	0	1	2	3
Capitals are not used improperly	0	1	2	3

Punctuation

Punctuation occurs at the end of each sentence	0	1	2	3
End punctuation is correct	0	1	2	3

Sentence Construction

Absence of run-on sentences	0	1	2	3
Absence of sentence fragments	0	1	2	3
Absence of nonsensical sentences	0	1	2	3

Paragraph Construction

Each paragraph contains a topic sentence	N/A	0	1	2	3
Each sentence within a paragraph relates to the topic sentence	N/A	0	1	2	3

Appearance of Written Product

Words are legible	N/A	0	1	2	3
Spacing is appropriate between letters/words	N/A	0	1	2	3
Margins are appropriate	N/A	0	1	2	3
Written product is neat, with correct spelling	N/A	0	1	2	3

TOTAL SCORE ____

QUALITY EVALUATION MEASURE FOR WRITTEN PRODUCTS— ELEMENTARY LEVEL

Student Name: _Cary_

Date: _4-21-10_

Grade: _5_

Rating Scale:

    3 =   Skill used consistently and accurately throughout written product (> 95% of time)

    2 =   Skill used frequently and accurately throughout written product (50–94% of time)

    1 =   Skill used infrequently or inaccurately (< 50% of the time)

    0 =   No evidence of skill

Capitalization

First words in sentences are capitalized		0	1	2	_3_
Proper nouns are capitalized		0	1	2	_3_
Capitals are not used improperly		0	1	2	_3_

Punctuation

Punctuation occurs at the end of each sentence		0	1	2	_3_
End punctuation is correct		0	1	2	_3_

Sentence Construction

Absence of run-on sentences		0	1	2	_3_
Absence of sentence fragments		0	1	2	_3_
Absence of nonsensical sentences		0	1	2	_3_

Paragraph Construction

Each paragraph contains a topic sentence	_N/A_	0	1	2	3
Each sentence within a paragraph relates to the topic sentence	_N/A_	0	1	2	3

Appearance of Written Product

Words are legible	_N/A_	0	1	2	3
Spacing is appropriate between letters/words	_N/A_	0	1	2	3
Margins are appropriate	_N/A_	0	1	2	3
Written product is neat, with correct spelling	_N/A_	0	1	2	3

TOTAL SCORE   _24_

Summary Form for Academic Assessment

Data obtained during Steps 1 and 2 represent the collection of extensive information about a student's present level of academic performance. The data also provide a means of examining the academic environment in which the student's problems are occurring. To facilitate the process of assembling these data, a form for summarizing these data (Form 12) is provided.

DATA SUMMARY FORM FOR ACADEMIC ASSESSMENT

Child's name: _____

Teacher: _____

Grade: _____

School: _____

School district: _____

Date: _____

READING—SKILLS

Primary type of reading series used

☐ Basal reader

☐ Literature-based

☐ Trade books

Secondary type of reading materials used

☐ Basal reader

☐ Literature-based

☐ Trade books

☐ None

Title of curriculum series: _____

Level/book—target student: _____

Level/book—average student: _____

Results of passages administered:

Grade level/ book	Location in book	WC/ min	Words incorrect/ min	% correct	Median scores for level			Learning level (M, I, F)
					WC	ER	%C	
	Beginning							
	Middle							
	End							
	Beginning							
	Middle							
	End							
	Beginning							
	Middle							
	End							
	Beginning							
	Middle							
	End							

(cont.)

READING—ENVIRONMENT

Instructional Procedures:

Primary type of reading instruction:

☐ Basal readers ☐ Whole-language

☐ Other (describe) _____

_____

Number of reading groups: _____

_____

Student's reading group (if applicable): _____

_____

Allotted time/day for reading: _____

_____

Contingencies: _____

_____

Teaching procedures: _____

_____

Observations: _____ None completed for this area

System used:

☐ BOSS

☐ Other _____

Setting of observations:

☐ ISW:TPsnt ☐ SmGp:Tled ☐ Coop

☐ ISW:TSmGp ☐ LgGp:Tled ☐ Other _____

BOSS results:

Target _____	Peer _____	Target _____	Peer _____
AET% _____	AET% _____	OFT-M% _____	OFT-M% _____
PET% _____	PET% _____	OFT-V% _____	OFT-V% _____
		OFT-P% _____	OFT-P% _____
	TDI% _____		

Intervention Strategies Attempted:

_____ Simple _____

_____

_____ Moderate _____

_____

_____ Intensive _____

_____

RESPONSE TO INTERVENTION—SPECIAL SECTION: READING

Does the school have a currently operating RTI model for reading?

☐ Yes ☐ No

Is this student assigned to tiered instruction beyond tier 1 for reading?

☐ Yes ☐ No

For how many years has the model been in place?

☐ Less than 1 year ☐ 1 year ☐ 2 years ☐ 3+ years

To which tier is the student currently assigned?

☐ Tier 1 ☐ Tier 2 ☐ Tier 3 ☐ Other_____

Describe the specific interventions that have been used at each tier.

Tier 1 _____

_____

Tier 2 _____

_____

Tier 3 _____

_____

What are the benchmark scores (and measures) for the student p, the current year?

Fall _____

Winter _____

Spring _____

What are the expected benchmark scores (and measures) for the student for the current year?

Fall _____

Winter _____

Spring _____

What is the student's rate of improvement (ROI) for progress monitoring?

Expected ROI _____

Targeted ROI _____

Attained ROI _____

TEACHER-REPORTED STUDENT BEHAVIOR

Rate the following areas from 1 to 5 (1 = very unsatisfactory, 3 = satisfactory, 5 = superior)

Reading Group

a. Oral reading ability (as evidenced in reading group) _____

b. Volunteers answers _____

c. When called upon, gives correct answer _____

d. Attends to other students when they read aloud _____

e. Knows the appropriate place in book _____

Independent Seatwork

a. Stays on task _____

b. Completes assigned work in required time _____

c. Work is accurate _____

d. Works quietly _____

e. Remains in seat when required _____

Homework (if any)

a. Handed in on time _____

b. Is complete _____

c. Is accurate _____

STUDENT-REPORTED BEHAVIOR   _____ None completed for this area

Understands expectations of teacher	☐ Yes	☐ No	☐ Not sure
Understands assignments	☐ Yes	☐ No	☐ Not sure
Feels he/she can do the assignments	☐ Yes	☐ No	☐ Not sure
Likes the subject	☐ Yes	☐ No	☐ Not sure
Feels he/she is given enough time to complete assignments	☐ Yes	☐ No	☐ Not sure
Feels like he/she is called upon to participate in discussions	☐ Yes	☐ No	☐ Not sure

MATH—SKILLS

Curriculum series used: _____

_____

Specific problems in math: _____

_____

Mastery skill of target student: _____

_____

Mastery skill of average student: _____

_____

Instructional skill of target student: _____

_____

Instructional skill of average student: _____

_____

Problems in math applications: _____

_____

Results of math probes:

Probe type	No.	Digits correct/min	Digits incorrect/min	% problems correct	Learning level (M, I, F)

Concepts–Applications	Number of correct responses	Percentage of problems correct

RESPONSE TO INTERVENTION—SPECIAL SECTION: MATH

Does the school have a currently operating RTI model for math?

☐ Yes   ☐ No

Is this student assigned to tiered instruction beyond Tier 1 for math?

☐ Yes   ☐ No

For how many years has the model been in place?

☐ Less than 1 year   ☐ 1 year   ☐ 2 years   ☐ 3+ years

To which tier is the student currently assigned?

☐ Tier 1   ☐ Tier 2   ☐ Tier 3   ☐ Other_____

Describe the specific interventions that have been used at each tier.

Tier 1 _____

Tier 2 _____

Tier 3 _____

What are the benchmark scores (and measures) for the student in the current year?

Fall _____

Winter _____

Spring _____

What are the expected benchmark scores (and measures) for the student in the current year?

Fall _____

Winter _____

Spring _____

What is the student's rate of improvement (ROI) for progress monitoring?

Expected ROI _____

Targeted ROI _____

Attained ROI _____

MATH—ENVIRONMENT

Instructional Procedures:

Number of math groups: _____

Student's group (high, middle, low): _____

Allotted time/day: _____

Teaching procedures: _____

Contingencies: _____

OBSERVATIONS: NONE COMPLETED FOR THIS AREA

System used:

- ☐ BOSS
- ☐ Other _____

Setting of observations:

- ☐ ISW:TPsnt   ☐ SmGp:Tled   ☐ Coop
- ☐ ISW:TSmGp   ☐ LgGp:Tled   ☐ Other _____

BOSS results:

Target	_____	Peer	_____	Target	_____	Peer	_____
A%	_____	AET%	_____	OFT-M%	_____	OFT-M%	_____
PET%	_____	PET%	_____	OFT-V%	_____	OFT-V%	_____
				OFT-P%	_____	OFT-P%	_____
		TDI%	_____				

Intervention Strategies Attempted:

_____ Simple _____

_____

_____ Moderate _____

_____

_____ Intensive _____

_____

TEACHER-REPORTED STUDENT BEHAVIOR

Rate the following areas from 1 to 5 (1 = very unsatisfactory, 3 = satisfactory, 5 = superior)

Math group (large)

a. Volunteers answers   _____

b. When called upon, gives correct answer   _____

c. Attends to other students when they give answers   _____

d. Knows the appropriate place in math book   _____

Math Group (small)

a. Volunteers answers _____

b. When called upon, gives correct answer _____

c. Attends to other students when they give answers _____

d. Knows the appropriate place in math book _____

Math Group (cooperative)

a. Volunteers answers _____

b. Contributes to group objectives _____

c. Attends to other students when they give answers _____

d. Facilitates others in group to participate _____

e. Shows appropriate social skills in group _____

Independent Seatwork

a. Stays on task _____

b. Completes assigned work in required time _____

c. Work is accurate _____

d. Works from initial directions _____

e. Works quietly _____

f. Remains in seat when required _____

Homework (if any)

a. Handed in on time _____

b. Is complete _____

c. Is accurate _____

STUDENT-REPORTED BEHAVIOR _____ None completed for this area

Understands expectations of teacher	☐ Yes	☐ No	☐ Not sure
Understands assignments	☐ Yes	☐ No	☐ Not sure
Feels he/she can do the assignments	☐ Yes	☐ No	☐ Not sure
Likes the subject	☐ Yes	☐ No	☐ Not sure
Feels he/she is given enough time to complete assignments	☐ Yes	☐ No	☐ Not sure
Feels like he/she is called upon to participate in discussions	☐ Yes	☐ No	☐ Not sure

SPELLING—SKILLS

Type of material used for spelling instruction:

☐ Published spelling series

Title of series _____

☐ Basal reading series

Title of series _____

☐ Teacher-made materials

☐ Other _____

Curriculum series (if applicable): _____

_____

Results of spelling probes:

Grade level of probe	Probe no.	LSC	% words correct	Median LSC for grade level	Level (M, I, F)
	1				
	2				
	3				
	1				
	2				
	3				
	1				
	2				
	3				
	1				
	2				
	3				

SPELLING—ENVIRONMENT

Instructional Procedures:

Allotted time/day: _____

Teaching procedures: _____

Contingencies: _____

Observations: _____ None completed for this area

System used:

☐ BOSS

☐ Other _____

Setting of observations:

☐ ISW:TPsnt   ☐ SmGp:Tled   ☐ Coop

☐ ISW:TSmGp   ☐ LgGp:Tled   ☐ Other _____

BOSS results:

Target ____	Peer ____	Target ____	Peer ____
AET% ____	AET% ____	OFT-M% ____	OFT-M% ____
PET% ____	PET% ____	OFT-V% ____	OFT-V% ____
		OFT-P% ____	OFT-P% ____
	TDI% ____		

Intervention Strategies Attempted:

____ Simple _____

_____

____ Moderate _____

_____

____ Intensive _____

_____

STUDENT-REPORTED BEHAVIOR   ____ None completed for this area

Understands expectations of teacher	☐ Yes	☐ No	☐ Not sure
Understands assignments	☐ Yes	☐ No	☐ Not sure
Feels he/she can do the assignments	☐ Yes	☐ No	☐ Not sure
Likes the subject	☐ Yes	☐ No	☐ Not sure
Feels he/she is given enough time to complete assignments	☐ Yes	☐ No	☐ Not sure
Feels like he/she is called upon to participate in discussions	☐ Yes	☐ No	☐ Not sure

WRITING—SKILLS

Types of writing assignments: _____

Areas of difficulty:

Content:
☐ Expressing thoughts
☐ Story length
☐ Story depth
☐ Creativity

Mechanics:
☐ Capitalization
☐ Punctuation
☐ Grammar
☐ Handwriting
☐ Spelling

Results of written expression probes:

Story starter	Words written	Instructional level?	Comments

WRITING—ENVIRONMENT

Instructional Procedures:

Allotted time/day: _____

Teaching procedures: _____

_____

Observations: _____ None completed for this area

System used:

☐ BOSS

☐ Other _____

Setting of observations:

☐ ISW:TPsnt   ☐ SmGp:Tled   ☐ Coop

☐ ISW:TSmGp   ☐ LgGp:Tled   ☐ Other _____

BOSS results:

Target _____   Peer _____   Target _____   Peer _____

A% _____   AET% _____   OFT-M% _____   OFT-M% _____

PET% _____   PET% _____   OFT-V% _____   OFT-V% _____

                                  OFT-P% _____   OFT-P% _____

                 TDI% _____

STUDENT-REPORTED BEHAVIOR

_____ None completed for this area

Understands expectations of teacher	☐ Yes	☐ No	☐ Not sure
Understands assignments	☐ Yes	☐ No	☐ Not sure
Feels he/she can do the assignments	☐ Yes	☐ No	☐ Not sure
Likes the subject	☐ Yes	☐ No	☐ Not sure
Feels he/she is given enough time to complete assignments	☐ Yes	☐ No	☐ Not sure
Feels like he/she is called upon to participate in discussions	☐ Yes	☐ No	☐ Not sure

STEP 3

Instructional Modification

IN SELECTING STRATEGIES FOR INSTRUCTIONAL MODIFICATION, one should conceptualize these strategies as on a continuum of complexity. As illustrated in Figure 14, strategies are viewed as simple, moderate, or intensive. At the level of simple strategies, the focus is on enhancing student motivation by altering the type of feedback given to student responses, altering the instructional presentation, or presenting other strategies that may impact the way in which the teaching process is proceeding. Two examples of these types of strategies are provided in Forms 13 and 14. Form 13 (regrouping checklist) provides a set of cues for a student to follow as he/she is completing problems of addition and subtraction with regrouping. This simple checklist offers students reminders of the sequential process needed in correctly completing problems of regrouping to the 10's column. Students can be taught to use this checklist as a way to sequence the instructional process. Form 14 (reading checklist) is a simple list of reminders for students to follow when they are struggling with understanding sentences. The checklist offers students an opportunity to manage their own instructional process.

When simple interventions are not sufficient to improve student performance, more moderate levels of interventions can be used. The existing instruction is enhanced by adding strategies that provide more focused intensity on specific instructional skill development. This level of focus and specificity can be achieved by teaching mini-lessons, altering the pace of instructional delivery, or providing techniques such as peer tutoring. One of the most effective peer-tutoring techniques is Peer Assisted Learning Strategies© (PALS) developed by Lynn and Doug Fuchs at Vanderbilt University (*kc.vanderbilt.edu/pals*). These strategies have been identified by both the What Works Clearinghouse (*ies.ed.gov/ncee/wwc*) and Best Evidence Encyclopedia (*www.bestevidence.org*) as top-rated programs with strong empirical support.

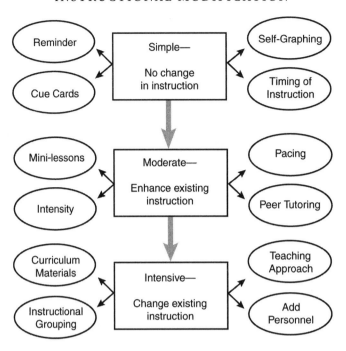

FIGURE 14. Levels of intervention development.

Many times, neither simple nor moderate levels of intervention result in the desired improvements in student performance. Strategies considered to be intensive may be needed; these often involve changes in instructional grouping, instructional materials, and/or methods of instruction. Resources that identify available strategies are plentiful. Some key resources that readers will find valuable can be found on web sites such as the Florida Center for Reading Research (*www.fcrr.org*), intervention central (*www.interventioncentral.org*), as well as in the practice guides published by the U.S. Department of Education, Institute for Education Sciences (*ies.ed.gov/ncee/wwc/publications/practiceguides*). The practice guides are especially important because the strategies provided in them are based on an evaluation of existing empirical evidence and can point users to the relative strength in research to support the recommended practices. In addition, some excellent print publications that provide intervention descriptions that can be recommended are books by Rathvon (2008; *Effective School Interventions: Evidence-Based Strategies for Improving School Outcomes*) as well as books by Shinn and Walker (2010; *Interventions for Achievement and Behavior Problems in a Three-Tier Model Including RTI*). These are just some of the many excellent resources available to support the selection and development of instructional modification strategies.

Presented here are two intervention strategies that have been found to be useful and powerful for practice in developing academic skills. The strategies can be applied broadly across skill areas.

REGROUPING CHECKLIST FOR ADDITION AND SUBTRACTION

Is the problem addition or subtraction?

Addition Checklist

☐ Add the 1's column.

☐ Is the answer more than 10?

 ☐ Put the 1's below the answer line.

 ☐ Put a 1 on top of the 10's column.

☐ Add the 10's column.

Subtraction Checklist

☐ Look at the 1's column.

☐ Can I subtract? Is the top number bigger than the bottom number? If NO:

 ☐ Go to the 10's and take away 1.

 ☐ Add the 10's to the 1's by placing a 1 in front of the top number.

☐ Subtract the 1's.

☐ Subtract the 10's.

FORM 14

CHECKLIST FOR SENTENCE CHECKING

Sentence Check . . . *"Did I understand this sentence?"*

If you had trouble understanding a word in the sentence, try . . .

☐ Reading the sentence over.

☐ Reading the next sentence.

☐ Looking up the word in the glossary (if the book or article has one).

☐ Asking someone.

If you had trouble understanding the meaning of the sentence, try . . .

☐ Reading the whole paragraph again.

☐ Reading on.

☐ Asking someone.

The Folding-In Technique

THE "FOLDING-IN" TECHNIQUE (also referred to as the "interspersal technique") has been found to be a powerful and easy-to-implement strategy that can be useful in any intervention whose objective is for a student to acquire new, fact-based information. The intervention can cut across subjects and can be used for anything from teaching students letter recognition in kindergarten, to word recognition, to multiplication facts, to events leading up to the Civil War, to chemical formulas.

Based upon the suggested ratios of Gickling's model of curriculum-based assessment (Gickling & Havertape, 1981), the procedure attempts to build success and momentum for acquisition of new information. By assessing a student's entry knowledge of the skill to be learned, the evaluator can determine the material a student already knows and the material that is unknown. When the new material is taught, the ratio of known to unknown material is maintained at no greater than 70% known and 30% unknown. Thus, a student who is being exposed to new material is never asked to try to learn more than 30% of what is presented.

The folding-in technique is based partly upon findings about the amount of repetition a student needs in order to master new information (Hargis, Terhaar-Yonker, Williams, & Reed, 1988). Learning is conceptualized as a process, as noted in Figure 15. In the acquisition stage, a student begins to be exposed to new material; in the mastery stage, the student becomes fluent with the material; and in the generalization and adaptation stages, the student discovers ways of applying the same or similar knowledge to novel situations. At an IQ level of 100, it takes approximately 35 repetitions for material to move from a level of acquisition to mastery. As the IQ goes up to 115, the number of repetitions decreases to about 15. At an IQ of 85, the number of repetitions increases to about 55 (Burns, 2001; Burns & Boice, 2009; MacQuarrie, Tucker, Burns, & Hartman, 2002). The folding-in technique is designed to maximize the number of repetitions to new material within a short period of time, thereby facilitating the student's progress from the acquisition to the mastery level of learning.

Level	Emphasis	Strategies
Acquisition	Achieving accurate responding	Demonstration, modeling, cues, prompting
Mastery	Accuracy with speed	Routine and novel drill and practice
Generalization	Performance and response under novel stimuli	Training discrimination and differentiation
Adaptation	Performance of similar responses under novel stimuli	Problem solving, role playing, training under simulation conditions

FIGURE 15. Stages of the learning process.

To illustrate the technique, it is described in detail for use in teaching word recognition and reading fluency as well as the acquisition of multiplication facts within a peer-tutoring context. Again, it is important for the reader to recognize that the technique can be applied to any content area where fact-based knowledge needs to be learned.

EXAMPLE: FOLDING-IN TECHNIQUE FOR WORD ACQUISITION AND READING FLUENCY

• **Step 1:** The evaluator selects a passage for the student to read. The passage should be one on which the student is currently working in class. It is important that the passage contain no more than 50% unknown material. This can be assessed by conducting a word search. The evaluator simply asks the student to read and explain the meaning of various key words from the passage. If the student misses more than 50% of the words in the word search, the evaluator should select a different passage and repeat the process.

• **Step 2:** The evaluator asks the student to read a portion of the passage (usually a paragraph or two) aloud and times the reading. The evaluator marks the point in the passage reached by the student at the end of 1 minute. The number of words read correctly in this minute is designated as the presession reading fluency.

• **Step 3:** As the student reads, the evaluator notes at least three words with which the student has difficulty or doesn't seem to understand. On 3″ × 5″ index cards, the evaluator writes the three words (one on each card). These words are designated as "unknowns." If more than three words can be designated as unknown, the evaluator selects words that are meaningful and helps the student to understand the story.

• **Step 4:** On 3″ × 5″ index cards, the evaluator writes seven words (one on each card) from the passage that the student does seem to know. These should be words that are meaningful to the passage, not simply *and, the,* or other nonmeaningful expressions.

- **Step 5:** The session begins with presentation of the first unknown word. The evaluator should define the word for the student and use it in a sentence. Next, the evaluator should ask the student to repeat the definition and use it in a different sentence.

- **Step 6:** Now the folding-in begins. After the unknown word is presented, one of the known words is presented. The student is asked to say the word aloud. Next, the unknown word is again presented, followed by the known word previously presented, and then a new known word. This sequence of presentation (unknown followed by known) is continued until all seven knowns and the one unknown word have been presented.

Next, the second unknown word is presented in the same way as the first, with the evaluator and then the student defining it and using it in a sentence. This second unknown word is then folded in among the other seven known words and the first unknown word. In the course of the multiple presentations of the words, the student is asked to repeat the unknown word's definition and to use it in a sentence whenever he/she hesitates or is incorrect in the pronunciation of the word. Finally, the third unknown is folded in among the other nine words (two unknown, seven known). Given that the other words were assessed to be known at the starting point, the student should not have any difficulty with these words. Figure 16 illustrates the full sequence of presentations for a set of 10 words.

- **Step 7:** Upon completion of the folding-in intervention, the student is asked to reread the passage. The evaluator again marks the number of seconds it took for the student to reach the point in the passage reached at 1 minute during the presession reading. It is important that the student read at least to the same point of the passage that he/she reached at the beginning of the session; this is necessary to establish accuracy in the oral reading rate measure. The score obtained here is considered the student's postsession reading score.

- **Step 8:** Both the pre- and postsession scores are graphed (usually by the student). These data can be very useful in showing the student the consistent improvement in his/her reading skills over the short period of time in each session, as well as the acquisition of material over days and weeks.

- **Step 9:** The next session begins by having the student read the next portion of the passage. Following the reading, the 10 words (seven known, three unknown) that were used in the previous session are reviewed. A mark is placed on one of the unknown words to designate that the student knew the word without hesitation during this session.

- **Step 10:** A criterion is set to determine when a previously unknown word is designated as a known word. Typically, this can be defined as getting the word correct on two consecutive sessions after it was introduced.

- **Step 11:** As a new unknown word is added to the drill procedure, one of the original known words is removed from the pile. The first word to be removed is one of the original known words selected on the first session. Each of the other seven known words is replaced with new unknown words. Finally, by the time one of the original unknown words is removed from the pile, it will have been drilled far in excess of the required 55 repetitions for new material to reach mastery levels.

Presentation no.	Unknown item no.	Known item no.
1	1	
2		1
3	1	
4		1
5		2
6	1	
7		1
8		2
9		3
10	1	
11		1
12		2
13		3
14		4
15	1	
16		1
17		2
18		3
19		4
20		5
21	1	
22		1
23		2
24		3
25		4
26		5
27		6
28	1	
29		1
30		2
31		3
32		4
33		5
34		6
35		7
36	2	
37	1	
38		1
39	2	
40	1	
41		1

Presentation no.	Unknown item no.	Known item no.
42		2
43		3
44	2	
45	1	
46		1
47		2
48		3
49		4
50	2	
51	1	
52		1
53		2
54		3
55		4
56		5
57	2	
58	1	
59		1
60		2
61		3
62		4
63		5
64		6
65	2	
66	1	
67		1
68		2
69		3
70		4
71		5
72		6
73		7
74	3	
75	2	
76	1	
77		1
78	3	
79	2	
80	1	
81		1
82		2

Presentation no.	Unknown item no.	Known item no.
83	3	
84	2	
85	1	
86		1
87		2
88		3
89	3	
90	2	
91	1	
92		1
93		2
94		3
95		4
96	3	
97	2	
98	1	
99		1
100		2
101		3
102		4
103		5
104	3	
105	2	
106	1	
107		1
108		2
109		3
110		4
111		5
112		6
113	3	
114	2	
115	1	
116		1
117		2
118		3
119		4
120		5
121		6
122		7

FIGURE 16. Sequences for presenting known and unknown materials in the folding-in technique, assuming 10 items (3 unknown and 7 known).

EXAMPLE: FOLDING-IN TECHNIQUE FOR MULTIPLICATION FACTS

Students: Two boys in third-grade special education class have been referred for problems in learning multiplication facts.

Preassessment Phase: To determine the number of known and unknown facts, the students are administered a quiz in which they are asked to answer all computational problems with fact families 1–9. The number of problems not completed or incorrect provides an indication of the facts that have and have not been learned.

Instructional Structure: The procedure is set up as a peer-tutoring activity. The students are taught the procedure and are required to conduct 10-minute tutoring sessions in which they drill each other using the folding-in technique.

- **Step 1:** Each student selects seven cards from his/her pile of preassessed known facts.
- **Step 2:** Each student selects one card from his/her pile of unknown preassessed facts.
- **Step 3:** The two students are informed by the teacher that they have 20 minutes to begin tutoring.
- **Step 4:** After it is decided which student will begin the tutoring, the folding-in procedure begins. The teacher of the pair presents the first unknown fact to the learner. The learner is required to write the fact on a piece of paper, say it to him-/herself three times, and then turn the paper over.
- **Step 5:** The teacher then presents a known fact, followed by the unknown fact, the first known fact, and another known fact. The unknown fact is presented sequentially in this fashion until all seven known facts have been presented and folded in among the unknown facts. (See Figure 16 for presentation sequence.)
- **Step 6:** The eight facts (one unknown and seven known) are shuffled. The second unknown fact is then presented and folded in among the other eight facts. This is repeated again for the third unknown fact.
- **Step 7:** If the student hesitates or is incorrect on any fact, the teacher instructs him/her to complete a brief correction procedure. The teacher tells him/her the correct answer and has him/her write the incorrect fact three times. The incorrect fact is then presented again to the learner.
- **Step 8:** When all facts have been folded in, the entire group of 10 facts is presented three times. Each time, the packet of index cards is shuffled to prevent the learner from simply remembering the sequence of responses.
- **Step 9:** The final step is a test of the 10 facts that the students have practiced. On this test, a mark is placed on the unknown fact cards if a student is correct on this trial. When an unknown fact attains three consecutive marks, it is considered to be a learned fact.
- **Step 10:** The number of new facts learned each week is graphed by the students. In addition, the teacher administers weekly curriculum-based measurement math probes taken from across all fact families. These data are also graphed.

Cover–Copy–Compare

THE "COVER–COPY–COMPARE" (CCC) technique has been found to be a simple but powerful technique for students who need practice and drill in moving skills from the stage of acquisition to mastery (see Figure 15). First described by Skinner and his colleagues for use in mastering multiplication facts in elementary students (Skinner, Turco, Beatty, & Rasavage, 1989), the technique has been applied to skill areas such as the learning of geography facts (Skinner, Belifore, & Pearce, 1992), science knowledge (Smith, Ditmer, & Skinner, 2002), and spelling (Erion, Davenport, Rodax, Scholl, & Hardy, 2009).

Despite changes in content, the basic technique is the same. Examining the technique as originally described by Skinner et al. (1989) for use in developing knowledge of basic multiplication facts in elementary-age students, the student first looks at a problem, covers the problem with an index card, writes the problem and solution in the next column, uncovers the problem and solution, and evaluates his/her response. The systematic nature of the practice offers an easily structured approach for students who need to rehearse and learn fact-based information, and it can be used by teachers, parents, or students themselves in almost any content area. In the area of mathematics facts, CCC worksheets can be easily generated by a computer program available from *interventioncentral.org*.

Two examples of the CCC technique are provided. Figure 17 is an example of a form useful for implementing CCC in math, in this case, for addition facts with sums to 18. Figure 18 is an adaptation of the CCC technique for spelling, in which the student views the word, covers the word, writes the word, and then evaluates his/her response. If incorrect, the student is instructed to write the word three times in the area provided.

Addition: Two one-digit numbers: Sums to 18.

Student: _____   Date: _____

Item 1: 2 CD/2 CD Total 8 + 9 **17**	8 + 9 CORRECT?
Item 2: 2 CD/2 CD Total 7 + 1 **8**	7 + 1 CORRECT?
Item 3: 2 CD/2 CD Total 6 + 1 **7**	6 + 1 CORRECT?
Item 4: 2 CD/2 CD Total 4 + 4 **8**	4 + 4 CORRECT?
Item 5: 2 CD/2 CD Total 6 + 1 **7**	6 + 1 CORRECT?
Item 6: 2 CD/2 CD Total 4 + 1 **5**	4 + 1 CORRECT?
Item 7: 2 CD/2 CD Total 7 + 8 **15**	7 + 8 CORRECT?
Item 8: 2 CD/2 CD Total 2 + 6 **8**	2 + 6 CORRECT?
Item 9: 2 CD/2 CD Total 5 + 4 **9**	5 + 4 CORRECT?

FIGURE 17. Example of a cover–copy–compare worksheet for addition facts to 18. CD, correct digits.

Write word	Cover	Copy	Compare
Leaf		Leaf	☺
Radiator		Radyator	Radiator x 3
Alligator		Aligatore	Alligatore x 3

Words I need to practice:

FIGURE 18. Sequences for presenting known and unknown materials in the folding-in technique, assuming 10 items (3 unknown and 7 known).

EXAMPLE: COVER–COPY–COMPARE FOR ADDITION FACTS, SUMS TO 18

- **Step 1:** Student examines the problem.
- **Step 2:** Student covers the problem with index card.
- **Step 3:** Student writes the problem and solution on the right side of the paper.
- **Step 4:** Student uncovers the problem and solution.
- **Step 5:** Student evaluates whether his/her written response matches the model.

EXAMPLE: COVER–COPY–COMPARE FOR SPELLING

- **Step 1:** Student examines the word.
- **Step 2:** Student covers the word with index card.
- **Step 3:** Student writes the word on the right side of the paper.
- **Step 4:** Student uncovers the word.
- **Step 5:** Student evaluates whether his/her written response matches the model.
- **Step 6:** If response is correct, move to next word; if response is incorrect, write three times.

Progress Monitoring

Graphing Data

ONE OF THE KEY COMPONENTS OF PROGRESS MONITORING is providing a visual display of the outcomes of the data-collection process. Such graphic displays serve to improve the evaluator's own understanding of the data; they also offer an effective mechanism for communicating with parents, teachers, and students themselves about student progress. Indeed, the process of collecting and reporting the data in a graphic form can itself serve as a strong motivator and reinforcement for some students.

Provided below are instructions for setting up hand-drawn graphs. However, technological advances suggest that evaluators should use existing graphing tools to display and manage the data. Although commercial software products for progress monitoring are available, such as AIMSweb® (*www.aimsweb.com*), DIBELS (*dibels. uoregon.edu*), and easyCBM (*easycbm.com*), among others, spreadsheet programs such as Microsoft Excel are common tools that can easily be used for graphing purposes. Resources using Microsoft Excel for progress monitoring graphs can be found on the Intervention Central website (*www.interventioncentral.org*).

SETTING UP GRAPHIC DISPLAYS

Graphic displays of data are useful for both short- and long-term monitoring. The setting-up process is similar for all types of graphs.

- **Step 1:** Identify the metric that is being used for data-collection purposes. This can be words correct or incorrect per minute, cumulative problems learned, number of pages mastered, number of homework problems done correctly, or other such measures.

• **Step 2:** Identify the possible range that the metric used for data collection can occupy. This can be any set of numbers representing the lower and upper limits that the measure is likely to attain.

• **Step 3:** The metric used for data collection becomes the range placed on the y (vertical) axis. Divide the range into equal units, and write these along the vertical axis.

• **Step 4:** Identify the amount of time across which the data will be collected. This can be any unit of time up to a full school year.

• **Step 5:** The amount of time for data collection becomes the range placed on the x (horizontal) axis. Divide the range into equal units (sessions, days, weeks, months, etc.).

The data are plotted by placing points on the graph, each of which indicates the outcome on the measure used for monitoring at each point in time when data are collected.

Graphs are usually divided by the particular phase of the intervention. Data obtained during baseline and intervention phases are separated by a solid line drawn on the graph. The data are also not connected by lines across these two phases. Once the intervention begins, changes in the intervention procedure are designated by broken lines, with the data again not being connected through those phases.

Figure 19 shows a graphic display for a first-grade student for whom two interventions—peer tutoring and peer tutoring plus curriculum-based measurement

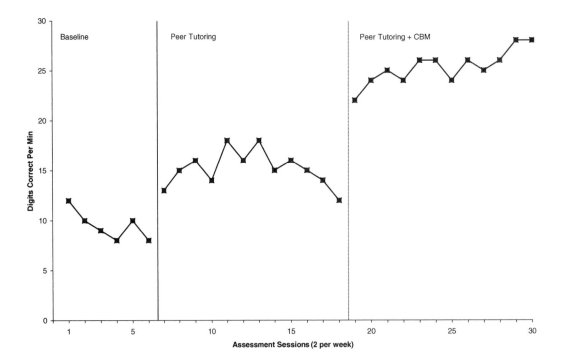

FIGURE 19. Example of math data for a first-grade student for whom peer tutoring and peer tutoring plus CBM were used as interventions.

(CBM) feedback—were implemented to improve performance on acquisition of basic math facts in addition and subtraction. The intervention operated for 15 weeks (one semester). Baseline and intervention phases are separated by a solid line, and the two intervention phases are separated by a broken line.

INTERPRETING GRAPHIC DATA

Deciding whether the data collected over time indicate that outcomes are moving in the expected direction can be done in several ways. Two of the most common methods of trend analysis are the quarter-intersect or split-middle method of White and Haring (1980), or the more mathematically precise method of calculating an ordinary least squares (OLS) trend line.

Quarter-Intersect (or Split-Middle) Method

To illustrate the first method of trend estimation, a step-by-step example is provided.

Figure 20 displays the data from the peer-tutoring phase (see Figure 19) of the intervention program described earlier, designed to improve the math computation performance of a first-grade student. To calculate a trend estimation, the following is done:

  • **Step 1:** Divide the entire data series of interest into two equal parts. If the number of data points is odd, then the middle data point of the series becomes the dividing line. If the number of data points is even, than the data series is split between the two middle points of the data series. In this example, there are 16 data points, so the series is split between the eighth and ninth data points (see Figure 20).
  • **Step 2:** Find the median score for each of the two sets of the data series. The median score is the middle or central score among the data points. If the middle score falls between two data points, then the median score is the halfway point between these two scores. In this example, there are eight data points in each half of the series. An examination of the data in the left half of the series shows that the score of 15.5 is the median score. The score for the right half of the data series is 15.5 (see Figure 20).
  • **Step 3:** Connect the median scores for each half of the data series (see Figure 20). This line represents the trend estimation for the data series.

Ordinary Least Squares Method

The OLS method generates a regression of the data points to a line that best fits the data series. Although OLS can be mathematically complex to calculate, software products such as Microsoft Excel contain a function that will allow the OLS to be calculated.

In practice, it is recommended that the OLS be used if it can be obtained, since research has shown it to be more accurate than other trend-line estimation

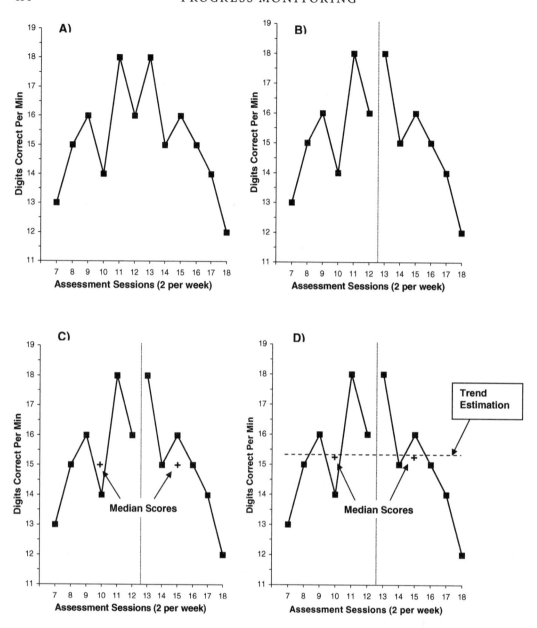

FIGURE 20. Illustration of the quarter-intersect or split-middle method of trend estimation for the peer-tutoring phase displayed in Figure 19.

methods, such as the quarter-intersect method. Figure 21 shows the results of the OLS calculated for the same data set as that used for the quarter-intersect method in Figure 20D.

OLS slope for Figure 21 was calculated as -0.08 words correct per minute/ assessment session. Typically, the slope of performance for progress monitoring is reported on a per week basis; since there were two assessment sessions per week, the overall slope in this example was -0.16 words correct per minute/week.

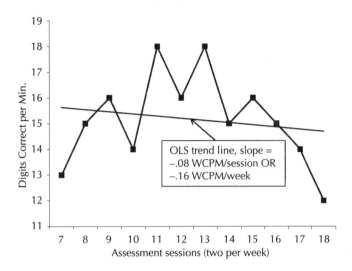

FIGURE 21. Illustration of the ordinary least squares (OLS) method of trend estimation for the peer tutoring displayed in Figure 20D.

PREPARING CBM-TYPE GRAPHS

The use of CBM requires that specific types of graphs be generated. These graphs provide opportunities to collect data across a long period of time (usually an entire school year), and to incorporate goal setting and graphing of expected performance. For example, Dan is a beginning third-grade student. Baseline data taken over 3 days show that Dan is reading at 48 words correct per minute (WCPM), 30 WCPM, and 53 WCPM in third-grade material. Using scores collected during a local norming project of Dan's school district, the teacher elects to set a yearly goal for Dan to read at the 50th percentile of third-grade readers by the end of the year—that is, a goal of 90 WCPM. Figure 22 shows the CBM graph generated. In the figure, Dan's baseline is represented by the median score across the three baseline data sessions (48 WCPM). A goal of 90 WCPM at the end of a 36-week period (one academic year from the time the data collection is started in September) is indicated on the graph, and a solid line connecting the baseline and goal is drawn. This line represents Dan's "aim line." As data are collected over time, it is anticipated that Dan's performance will match this line of progress. If his scores consistently exceed the aim line, then the teacher may decide to increase the goal originally set for Dan. If his scores are consistently below the aim line or move in a direction opposite to that shown by the aim line, the teacher should decide to alter the instructional technique to improve Dan's performance. Also, with the goal of 90 WCPM, Dan is expected to improve his oral reading fluency by 1.2 WCPM each week; this is his slope of targeted rate of improvement (90 WCPM – 48 WCPM = 42 WCPM ÷ 36 weeks = 1.2 WCPM/week).

Exercise 13 provides an opportunity to practice developing a CBM graph.

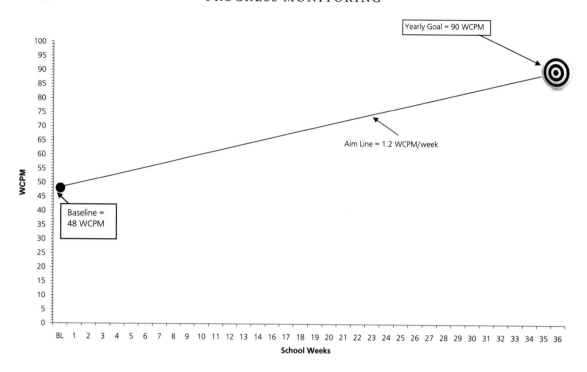

FIGURE 22. CBM graph showing Dan's baseline performance and expected rate of progress in reading across a school year.

DEVELOPING A CBM GRAPH

STUDENT

Betsy is a beginning fourth grader. Her reading fluency at baseline is determined to be 40 WCPM in fourth-grade material, where she will be taught this year. Her teacher, looking to set a goal that would place her at least at the 25th percentile for fourth graders at the end of the year, selects 88 WCPM as her year-end goal. Biweekly monitoring of her reading performance is planned across the 36 weeks of the school year.

DATA

During the first 5 weeks of school, the teacher obtains the following data:

Week 1:	45 WCPM
	35 WCPM
Week 2:	50 WCPM
	46 WCPM
Week 3:	50 WCPM
	44 WCPM
Week 4:	48 WCPM
	56 WCPM
Week 5:	52 WCPM
	55 WCPM

INSTRUCTIONS

1. Construct a graph including an aim line.

2. Plot Betsy's actual performance.

3. Use the quarter-intersect method to plot a trend estimation for Betsy's performance.

4. What might be the teacher's decision, based on these data?

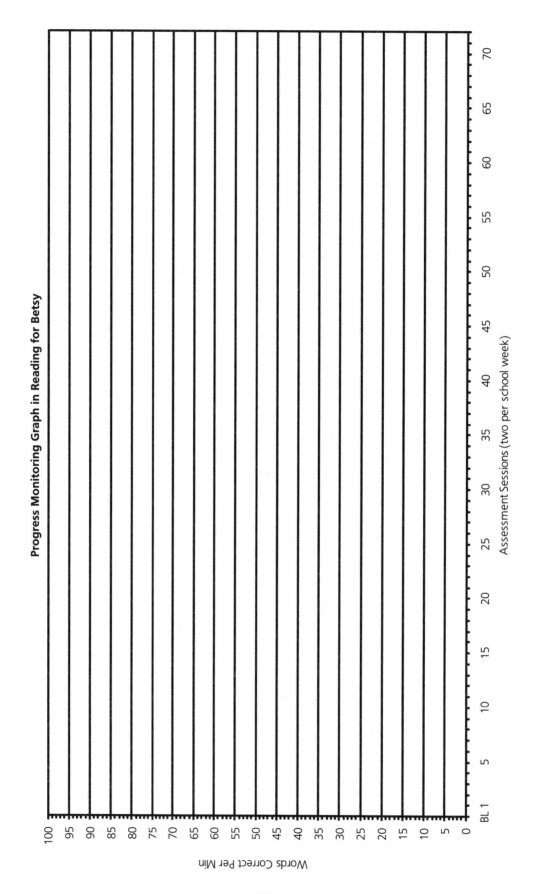

Progress Monitoring Graph in Reading for Betsy

Words Correct Per Min

Assessment Sessions (two per school week)

154

ANSWER FOR EXERCISE 13

The results of graphing Betsy's performance is shown in Figure 23. Trend lines using the quarter-intersect and the OLS methods are shown in Figure 24. In Betsy's case, both methods were approximately equal in showing her progress, which was found to be 1.4 WCPM/session or 2.8 WCPM/week (two assessment sessions per week). Looking at Figure 25, the data show that Betsy is making greater progress

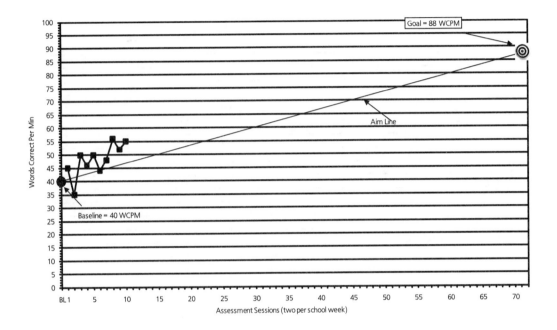

FIGURE 23. Progress monitoring graph for Betsy.

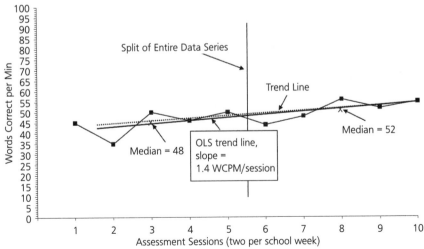

FIGURE 24. Quarter-intersect and OLS trend estimation for Betsy's reading progress.

than would her targeted ROI (target ROI = [88 − 40]/36 weeks = 1.3 WCPM/week). As such, it is possible that the goal set for her is currently too low. The teacher may decide to reset the goal for Betsy to 98 rather than 88 WCPM. When the new goal line is drawn, a dashed vertical line is used, and the new aim line, using a goal of 98 WCPM from the starting point (the baseline of 40 WCPM) is drawn between the dashed vertical line and the goal. Figure 26 shows the resulting CBM graph with the increased goal.

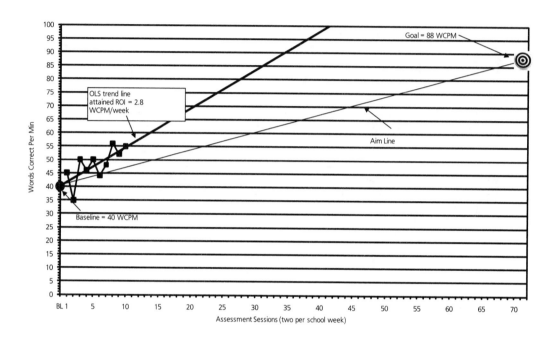

FIGURE 25. Betsy's CBM graph with OLS trend line.

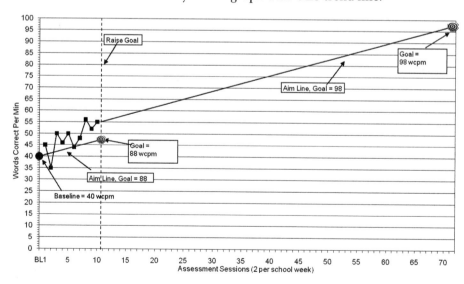

FIGURE 26. CBM graph for Betsy, with goal raised from 88 to 98 WCPM.

Developing Local Norms

THE PROCESS OF SELECTING GOALS IN CBA can be greatly enhanced by the use of local norms. Given that many schools and school districts are conducting universal screening as part of efforts to establish early intervention and the implementation of Response to Intervention (RTI) models, local norms are often already available from these data. However, in districts wishing to develop local norms where screening is not present, well-developed methods for doing so are available. Shinn (1988, 1989) provides an excellent discussion of this process and offers step-by-step directions on how to construct these norms. Specifically, Shinn (1988) notes that one must (1) create a measurement net that defines the appropriate skills and materials for assessment, (2) establish a normative sampling plan, (3) train data collectors, (4) collect the data, and (5) summarize the data. Gathering data that represent the performance of students within the schools where the data will be used provides a strong sense of ownership of the outcomes, and increases the certainty that the data comparison will be representative of the community.

To illustrate this process, the steps involved in the collection of local norms in reading for elementary school students from a medium-size urban school district are described. Readers should note that the sampling procedures used here are different from those recommended by Shinn (1988). The normative data from three districts are also presented, each representing high, moderate, and low levels of socioeconomic status, as defined by the percentage of low-income families in the district.

CREATING THE MEASUREMENT NET

Schools typically use already developed reading passages for purposes of norming or universal screening. These passages have been carefully calibrated for grade-level readability. Such passages are commercially available in products such as AIMSweb®

or DIBELS, among others. The advantage of using these passages is that students have not typically come in contact with them, thus avoiding any practice effects from repeated reading. In addition, the passages are well controlled for readability so that difficulty level across passages is less likely to result in differences in student performance within grade levels.

Although many school districts develop norms using these generic reading passages, the particular school district presented as an example at the time of the norm development wanted to use its own reading series to conduct the norms. Data were collected three times during the year: fall (October), winter (February), and spring (May). Reading levels of average students within grades were inconsistent across the district. At some schools, students were reading at levels commensurate with the publisher's assessment of grade level of the material; in other schools, the majority of students were reading approximately one level (or book) behind. When this discrepancy was discussed, the school district decided to use the publisher-recommended grade-level material as the measures to be assessed. Passages for assessment were taken from materials that constituted the end-of-year goals for students in each grade, and each passage selected was evaluated using the Spache readability formula. Only passages that had readability levels within the grade-level book from which the passage was taken were used (see Table 3).

Randomly selected passages of between 150 and 200 words were selected from each book, according to standard CBM procedures. Passages were retyped on separate pages for presentation.

SELECTING THE SAMPLE

When districts are conducting universal screening, the selection of the sample is not of concern since the entire school population is being assessed. However, when local norms are being collected and not all schools are involved in the data-collection process, issues of sample selection become very important. Given the size of the school district and resources available for data collection in the example presented here, it was not possible simply to select students randomly from across the district, as is often recommended in the process of obtaining local norms. In addition, the school district included a wide range of socioeconomic and academic ability levels that needed to be equally represented in the sample.

TABLE 3. **Measurement Net in Reading for Norming**

Grade	Name of book	Publisher's assigned grade level
1	*Surprise*	1.4[a]
2	*Friends*	2.1[b]
3	*Just Listen*	3.1[b]
4	*Dinosauring*	4
5	*Explore*	5

[a]Indicates fourth book of grade level.
[b]Indicates first book of grade level.

To address the problems of the resources available to collect the data, it was decided to concentrate the normative sample on six elementary schools. In considering the wide range of socioeconomic levels, the school district administrators identified six schools, two each that represented lower (L), lower-middle (LM), and middle (M) socioeconomic levels (the three levels characterizing the district). To validate the selection of these schools, the percentages of students on free or reduced-fee lunches in the three schools were compared. The L schools identified had 93% of the students on free or reduced-fee lunches; the LM schools had 56%; and the M schools had 23%. Thus, these schools appeared to accurately represent the range of socioeconomic levels in the district.

The next problem was to develop a sample that would fairly represent the range of reading abilities within each of these schools. To accomplish this, prior to each scheduled assessment, the reading specialist assigned to each school provided a list of the current placement within the reading series of all students in that building. These data were used to identify the proportion of students in each grade within a building at each level of the reading series. For example, in the L schools, it was found that in the third grade, 10% of the students were reading in *Dinosauring* (fourth-grade book), 30% were reading in *Just Listen* (first book of third grade), 50% were reading in *Friends* (first book of the second grade), 8% were reading in *Surprises* (fourth book of the first grade), and 2% were reading below the first-grade level.

A normative sample consisting of 900 students was developed, representing approximately 25% of the population in the three schools. From each school, 150 students (30 per grade) were selected. The normative sample within each school was constructed by selecting the identical proportion of students from each level of the reading series within each grade within each school. For example, to select the students from the third grade in the L school, the list of students placed in the *Just Listen* book was obtained. As noted earlier, this represented 30% of the third-grade students. Given that the final sample from the third grade of the L schools would have 30 students, a total of 4 (15% of 30) would be selected at random from among the possible 15% for inclusion in the normative sample. This process was repeated for each grade level and each school, in order to end up with a final sample whose representation was proportional to the percentage of students at the various reading levels of the grade.

DATA COLLECTION

Data were collected over 2-week periods in October, February, and May during the school year. Graduate students in school psychology and special education served as data collectors. Students were tested on an individual basis in a small room adjacent to the classrooms in each of the school buildings. Each student was asked to read a passage aloud and was timed for 1 minute. The number of words read correct per minute was calculated according to standard CBM techniques. Errors included mispronunciations, omissions, and substitutions.

DATA ANALYSIS AND RESULTS

Results obtained from the normative data collection can be displayed in numerous ways. Table 4 and Figure 27 show the overall outcomes for the entire district. Such data as these can be used as benchmarks for a district's expectations and performance.

    An important concern in using local norms is a recognition that a district's overall level of academic performance is likely to vary considerably based on the overall socioeconomic base of the district. Table 5 provides data from three districts where local norms were collected. One of the districts has a high number of low-income families (59.5%), the second a moderate level of low-income families (32.8%), and the third a small number of low income families (6.3%). As can be seen in Table 5, reading performance varied greatly across these districts. For example, students assessed in the spring of the third grade, who scored at the 25th percentile, ranged from 44 WCPM in the low-income district, 89 WCPM in the moderate-income district, and 102 WCPM in the high-income district. Although the differences lessened as students reached the fifth-grade level, there was still a difference of 33 WCPM between the low- and high-income districts. Clearly, using local norms places students' performance within the context of the environment in which they are living. Using data such as those in Table 5 can allow a district to set ambitious goals that may challenge students to reach levels of performance similar to those districts that may have high-percentages of high-achieving students.

TABLE 4. Quartiles for Local Norms in Reading from Grade-Level Reading Material for a Medium-Size Urban District in the Northeastern United States

Grade	Percentile	Fall	Winter	Spring
1	25th	1	2	6
	50th	2	5	13
	75th	6	15	35
2	25th	11	21	31
	50th	26	38	53
	75th	38	74	85
3	25th	36	38	44
	50th	50	63	78
	75th	81	95	118
4	25th	53	59	75
	50th	73	81	92
	75th	98	110	120
5	25th	77	83	88
	50th	98	110	121
	75th	130	142	151

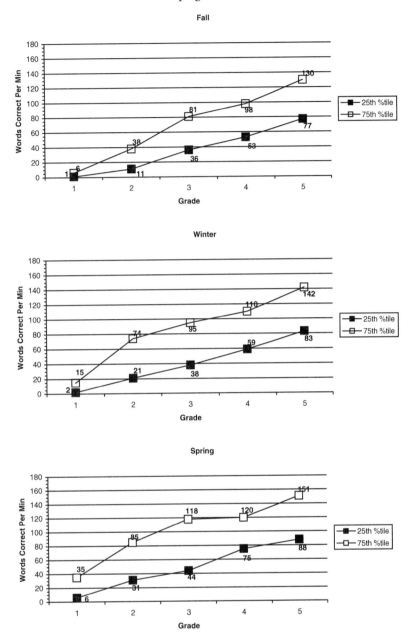

FIGURE 27. Normative data in reading from midsize urban school district showing 25th and 75th percentiles across grades and assessment periods.

TABLE 5. Words Correct per Minute Scores at the 25th Percentile across Three School Districts from High, Moderate, and Low Socioeconomic Bases

	Fall	Winter	Spring
Grade 1			
High	4	29	59
Moderate	4	15	26
Low	1	2	6
Grade 2			
High	31	69	79
Moderate	31	55	67
Low	11	21	31
Grade 3			
High	68	86	102
Moderate	62	77	89
Low	36	38	44
Grade 4			
High	80	98	114
Moderate	83	96	104
Low	53	59	75
Grade 5			
High	103	113	121
Moderate	90	101	115
Low	77	83	88

Although the example presented here used reading material that was from the district's curriculum of instruction, it is neither required nor recommended that districts develop their own passages for norming purposes. Standard reading passages that are closely controlled for grade-based readability are available from both commercial and free sites. Readers may want to examine these sources for reading passages that have been found to be effective in conducting local norms in reading. Such passages are available commercially from several sources, such as AIMSweb (*www.aimsweb.com*), DIBELS (*dibels.uoregon.edu*; *www.diebels.org*), Scholastic Fluency (*teacher.scholastic. com*), edcheckup (*www.edcheckup.com*), Read Naturally (*readnaturally.com*), and STEEP (*www.isteep.com*), among others. Materials for assessing prereading skills of emerging readers that include oral reading fluency passages up through sixth grade are also available (AIMSweb, DIBELS). Also, Hasbrouck and Tindal (2006) have compiled a set of norms from multiple norming projects that can provide reasonable estimates of normative performance for most school districts and are publicly available at *www.readnaturally.com/pdf/oralreadingfluency. pdf.*

Using Goal Charts

Once schools have selected their norms, whether using those commercially available from such sources as AIMSweb®, those available from Hasbrouck and Tindal (2006) (*www.readnaturally.com/pdf/oralreadingfluency.pdf*), or locally created, evaluators can use these data both to establish a student's current level of performance and to set a goal for expected performance. A tool that assists in goal setting is the use of goal charts. A goal chart plots the average student performance from the 25th to the 75th percentile for each grade, a range that represents the instructional level. When the performance of the student is plotted on the chart, the outcome shows the contrast between the reading level of the target student and the expected reading level for each student across each grade in which the student was assessed. These charts can be useful for goal setting when progress monitoring is being conducted below the student's grade level.

Figure 28 shows an example of a goal chart for a student based on the fall assessment. The district decided to use the normative data provided by the AIMSweb database. The student, a third grader, was first tested in third-grade materials, where he was found to be reading at 35 WCPM. This was substantially below the 25th percentile for same-grade peers who were reading 49 WCPM. When tested in second-grade materials, he was found to be reading 45 WCPM—well within the 25th percentile of other second-grade students. In first-grade material he was found to be reading at 60 WCPM, which was well above the 75th percentile band of comparison for first-grade students in his district. Based on the analysis of his data, the decision was made that he was instructional in the second-grade level (between the 25th and 75th percentiles), which would be the level of material in which he would be monitored and taught.

To set a reasonable goal using the goal chart, the evaluator would examine what level the student would need to reach by the middle of the school year (winter) to attain at least the 50th percentile of performance for the grade level where monitoring and instruction will occur. The overall objective for the year is to try to

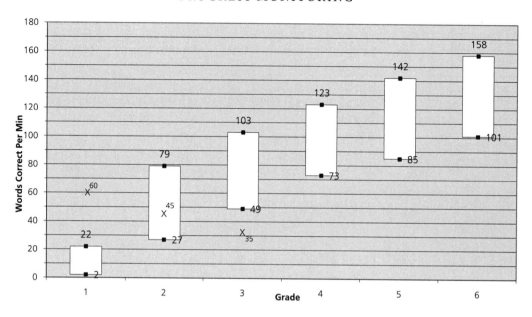

FIGURE 28. Goal chart for reading at fall for a third grader.

move the student as fast as possible to monitoring and instruction consistent with his/her grade level. Using the goal chart for second-grade students as seen in figure 29, a goal of 75 WCPM by the middle of the year in second grade material was set. The targeted rate of improvement (ROI) is 1.7 WCPM/week, calculated by subtracting the goal minus the current rate and dividing by 18 weeks (approximately half a school year).

Assuming he/she achieves this goal by midyear, the evaluator would again assess the student's reading skills at third grade material. When this is done, the student is found to be reading at 70 WCPM in third-grade material. As seen in figure 30, the student's performance, plotted against the third-grade goal chart, indicates that he/she is just above the 25th percentile for the middle of third grade, placing the student within the instructional level. A goal is selected to maintain the student at approximately the 30th percentile for third-grade material to the end of year, which requires a performance of 90 WCPM by spring. The targeted ROI is 1.1 WCPM/week (90 WCPM – 70 WCPM/18 weeks). The decision not to accelerate the student's performance beyond the percentile attained in the third-grade material is based on the fact that the student had been moved up from second- to third-grade material during the year, and accelerating the student beyond that level was viewed by the team to be far too challenging.

Goal charts, such as those shown in Figures 28, 29, and 30, can be easily developed using graphing and spreadsheet programs such as Microsoft Excel.

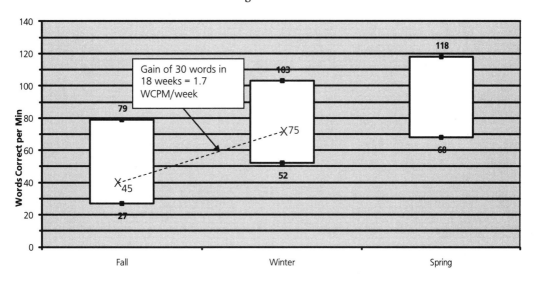

FIGURE 29. Goal chart for reading, setting fall to winter goal for third grader monitored at second-grade level.

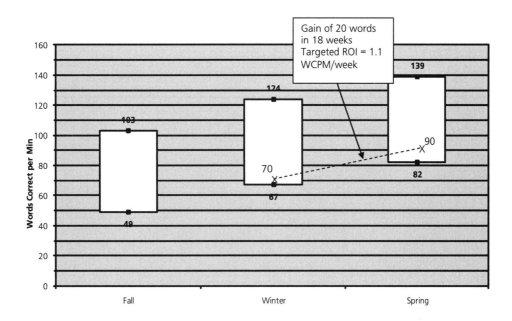

FIGURE 30. Goal chart for reading, setting winter to spring goal for third-grade students moved from second- to third-grade level.

Tools for Response to Intervention: Data-Based Decision Making

The 2004 REAUTHORIZATION of the Individuals with Disabilities Educational Improvement Act (IDEA) introduced response to intervention (RTI) as an alternative method to the well-known process of determining the discrepancy between a student's ability and his/her achievement as the basis for the identification of specific learning disabilities. Specifically, IDEA allows that a process which determines if students respond to scientific, research-based intervention can be used as an alternative to the well-known ability–achievement discrepancy. When using RTI for determining a specific learning disability (SLD), one needs to show substantial differences between the referred student and similar age/grade peers in both level of performance and the rate at which they improve when provided with instructional interventions known to be highly effective when implemented with strong integrity.

Perhaps more importantly than its methodology for determining the presence of an SLD, RTI is viewed as a system of prevention and early intervention focused on improving student academic skills or behavior. The processes that are considered to be key components of RTI form a framework for schoolwide implementation of effective services to all students. Without these processes in place, one could not use the RTI model as a means of identifying students with an SLD. Likewise, schools that choose not to use the RTI model for purposes of identifying SLD could still be implementing an RTI model as a means of delivering effective instructional services to all children in both general and special education (Fuchs, 2003; National Association of State Directors of Special Education, 2006; Vaughn, Wanzek, Woodruff, & Linan-Thompson, 2007).

All models of RTI consist of a common set of characteristics that include a multi-tiered approach to intervention (Marston, Muyskens, Lau, & Canter, 2003), universal screening of all students (Fuchs, 2003; Gresham, 2002), small-group and multi-tiered instruction delivered to students according to their skill needs (Brown-Chidsey & Steege, 2010; Brown-Chidsey, Bronaugh, & McGraw, 2009; Vaughn, Linan-Thompson, & Hickman, 2003), team structures to manage and analyze data collected through the process, and progress monitoring of student performance to assess the impact of interventions (Marston et al., 2003; Shapiro, Hilt-Panahon, & Gischlar, in press). Among these components, the effective collection, use, and interpretation of data related to student performance lie at the heart of the model.

Models of RTI vary somewhat by the context in which they are implemented. In some high-performing schools, implementers of the model need to consider how to effectively accommodate the large number of general education students who are highly proficient, allowing these students to reach levels beyond the expectations of typical grade-level performers. Likewise, in low-performing schools, implementers need to consider how to address the large numbers of general education students who are below grade-level expectations, while also providing effective interventions for those students who are at serious risk for failure. Regardless of the context of the model, however, all RTI models are driven by data-based decision making. Educator opinion and perceptions, although still important, must be supported by data as the underlying basis of the perspective. The entire school culture is driven by the outcomes, which are shown via the collection of data on student performance.

To effectively implement a data-based decision-making process, schools need tools. Each school will find the data tools that work best in that particular context. Here I provide a variety of tools found to be useful in clinical practice across multiple effective RTI implementations. Each tool is presented consistent with the components of the data-based decision-making process. Specifically, tools are provided to evaluate the fidelity of implementation of data-based decision-making meetings, to assist in the setting of grade-based group goals for student performance, and to assist in making data-based individual decisions. The tools presented here are specifically for reading within the elementary school level, which is where the most frequent models of RTI implementation are found. Additional tools relevant to RTI implementation across academic skill areas can be found in Shapiro, Zigmond, Wallace, and Marston (in press).

LEVELS OF IMPLEMENTATION—DATA ANALYSIS

The data analysis process within RTI models is facilitated by teams. Typically, two levels of teams are present in RTI implementations, although some schools may combine these two teams into a single unit. The *core team* includes on-site key professionals with skills and passion for data analysis and could potentially include anyone working in that school (school psychologists, counselors, general education teachers, special education teachers, intervention specialists). Core teams usually have responsibilities that cut across grades and are headed by the school's senior leadership, such as the principal or assistant principal. The core team often makes initial recommendations for student assignment to intervention groups based on its analysis of the data. The core team also usually sets the grade-level goals related to student outcomes and considers the strategies that are needed at the level of the core program (Tier 1) to ensure overall student success. Considerations of the implementation fidelity of overall instruction as well as the effectiveness of identified interventions at Tiers 2 and 3 are a part of the team's responsibilities.

The *grade-level* team usually consists of all teaching staff at the specific grade level. Included would be those providing remedial support in programs such as Title I (i.e., federally funded remedial programs), special education, and intervention specialists. At grade-level meetings, the recommendations of the core team are presented, with the grade-level team having the opportunity to counter the core team's decision. Any alteration to the core team decision must be based on data brought to the team by the grade-level staff. Examination of progress monitoring data for those students currently in Tier 2 or 3, as well as other data collected as part of the RTI process (curriculum-embedded tests such as end-of-level or unit tests) are discussed and decisions on student tier placement are finalized. Implementation fidelity of the interventions are also part of the discussion.

Forms 15 and 16 provide checklists that can be used to determine the steps that core teams and grade-level teams should be following.

GRADE-LEVEL GROUP GOAL SETTING

One of the key principles within RTI models is that the percentage of students reaching proficiency or benchmarks should be at least around 70% of the students in the grade. Universal screening data are typically collected three times per year (fall, winter, spring), and these data are used to determine and set the goals for the subsequent benchmark period within the year. Given that many schools do not begin the year at the 70% level of proficiency across grades, one of the first responsibilities of the core team is to examine the percentage of students at benchmark in each grade at each assessment point and establish what would be reasonable but challenging goals for the grade as a group to reach at the next benchmark level. Achieving the goals set requires that strategies be implemented within the core instructional program that will maximize the learning outcomes for all students. Discussion of such strategies, including a mechanism to examine the fidelity with which these strategies are put in place, also is a part of the core team's focus.

Several tools can be used to support the setting of grade-level group goals. In order to move students who are currently below benchmark to levels at or above benchmark at the next assessment period, one must accelerate the rate of students' performance above the level that typically performing students would advance. In other words, when one looks at the universal screening data, one determines what level of performance attained by a third grader in the fall must be reached in winter if he/she were to stay at benchmark. For example, when using the benchmarks established by DIBELS (see Table 6), one can see that a third grader in the fall would be reading at 77 WCPM and would need to be at 92 WCPM at winter, 18 weeks later. The rate of improvement (ROI) for this typical student would be 0.8 WCPM/week (92 − 77/18 weeks). For a student below benchmark to "catch up" and move from strategic to benchmark levels, he/she would need to move at a rate greater than 0.8 WCPM/week. Based on the work of Fuchs, an ambitious level of change would be somewhere between one and a half and two times the typical rate. We have found that a rate of one and a half times the typical rate works well in setting

TABLE 6. DIBELS Benchmarks and Rate of Improvement across Grades across the School Year

Measure	Fall	Winter (fall–winter ROI)	Spring (winter–spring ROI)	Total year ROI
K-ISF	8	25 (0.9)	N/A	
K-PSF	0	18 (1.0)	35 (0.9)	1.0
K-NWF	0	13 (0.7)	25 (0.7)	0.7
1—NWF	24	50 (1.4)	50 (NA)	0.7
1—ORF	0	20 (1.1)	40 (1.1)	1.1
2	44	68 (1.3)	90 (1.2)	1.3
3	77	92 (0.8)	110 (1.0)	0.9
4	93	105 (0.7)	118 (0.7)	0.7
5	104	115 (0.6)	124 (0.5)	0.6

reasonable yet ambitious group goals. Thus, one would select a rate of 1.2 WCPM/ week ($0.8 \times 1.5 = 1.2$) as the targeted ROI for the group.

Using Form 17 (instructions for Form 17 are provided on page 183), the core team can set the goals for moving students from strategic to benchmark in their performance for the next assessment period. An illustration of the process is provided in Figure 31, based on the data from Figure 32.

- **Step 1:** The DIBELS ROI for moving from fall to winter for students reaching benchmark levels is 0.7 WCPM/week. This value is placed in the box under Step 1.
- **Step 2:** The target ROI is calculated by multiplying the typical ROI by the rate of acceleration—in this case, 1.5—which equals 1.05 or rounded to 1.1 WCPM/ week.
- **Step 3:** The expected gain in number of words is calculated by multiplying the targeted ROI by the number of weeks until the next benchmark assessment (usually 18 weeks, half of a school year). In this case the calculation is $1.1 \times 18 = 19.8$ words, rounded to 20.
- **Step 4:** The benchmark target for the next assessment period is first identified. Using the DIBELS benchmarks in this example, as seen in Table 6, the winter benchmark for students in fourth grade is 104 WCPM. This score is subtracted from the expected gain score, resulting in what is called the *cutoff score*. In this case the cutoff score is 84 (104 – 80). The cutoff score represents the students who, if their rate of performance accelerated between fall and winter at the targeted ROI, would likely reach benchmark at the winter assessment.
- **Step 5:** The number of students who is within the strategic range but at or above the cutoff score of 84 is determined. Looking at the data displayed in Figure 32, there are a total of 5 students between scores of 80 and 92. If one looked at the exact distribution of the scores between 80 and 89, one would find that 4 of the 5 students would be between 84 and 92. A total of 24 students are currently at benchmark (see Figure 32), resulting in a total predicted number of students at benchmark by winter of 28.
- **Step 6:** The number of students predicted to be at benchmark is divided by the total number of students in the grade—in this case, 38—resulting in a goal of 74% of students at benchmark by the winter assessment.

GOAL-SETTING WORKSHEET: STRATEGIC TO BENCHMARK

1. Determine the typical rate of improvement (ROI; look at the AIMSweb or DIBELS benchmark sheet).

Typical Rate of Improvement:
0.7

2. Determine target ROI (multiply the typical ROI by 1.5).

*0.7*_____ (Typical ROI) × **1.5** (Multiplier) = _*1.05*_____ (Target ROI)
*0.7*_____ × *1.5*_____ = *1.06*_____ ≈ *1.1*

3. Determine expected gain (EG).
   a. Multiply the target ROI (your result from Step 2) by the number of weeks till the next benchmark assessment (typically this is an 18-week period).
   b. This is the number of words you expect the students to gain in the coming benchmark period.

*1.1*_____ (Typical ROI) × _*18*_____ (Number of weeks) = _*19.8*_____ (EG)
*1.1*_____ × *18*_____ = *19.8*_____ ≈ *20*

4. Calculate the cutoff score.
   a. Find the benchmark target for the next assessment period.
   b. Subtract your number from Step 3 from the next benchmark target.
   c. This gives you the cutoff score.

*104*_____ (Next benchmark target) − _*20*_____ (EG) = _*84*_____ (Cutoff score)
*104*_____ − *20*_____ = *84*_____

5. Determine how many students you can expect to get to benchmark. Determine how many students at the strategic level are at or above the cutoff number (the number you determined in Step 4).
   a. Look at the distribution.
   b. Find the cutoff score in the graph.
   c. Count how many students are at or above that cutoff score. (Remember to count the number of students who are already at benchmark as well.)

Strategic students at or above cutoff number: _*4*_____
Number of students already at benchmark: _*24*_____
Total number of students expected to be at benchmark by next assessment: _*28*_____

6. Convert the number of students you expect to reach or stay at benchmark in time for the next assessment into a percentage:
   a. Divide the number of students from Step 5 by the total number of students at the grade level and multiply by 100.
   b. This is the percentage of students you expect to reach benchmark in the next assessment . . . your goal!

*28*_____ (Total: Step 5) ÷ _*38*_____ (Total # of students) = _*.74*_____ × 100 = _*74*_____ %
*28*_____ ÷ *38*_____ = *.74*_____ × 100 = *74*_____ %
Goal for next assessment: _*74*_____ %

FIGURE 31. Example of data for goal setting in the fall for a fourth-grade class.

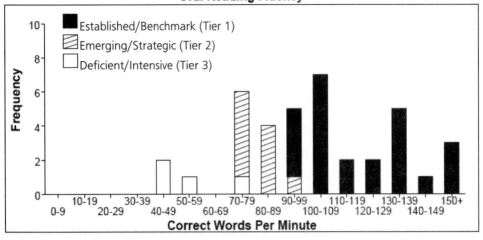

	0-9	10-19	20-29	30-39	40-49	50-59	60-69	70-79	80-89	90-99	100-109	110-119	120-129	130-139	140-149	150+
Deficient	0	0	0	0	2	1	0	1	0	0	0	0	0	0	0	0
Emerging	0	0	0	0	0	0	0	5	4	1	0	0	0	0	0	
Established	0	0	0	0	0	0	0	0	0	4	7	2	2	5	1	3

	Description	Target Range (WCPM)	Ns	%s
☐	Deficient/Intensive (Tier 3)	< 71	4	11%
▨	Emerging/Strategic (Tier 2)	71 – 92	10	26%
■	Established/Benchmark (Tier 1)	93+	24	63%

Goals for next benchmark

	Next Benchmark:	Target Range (WCPM)	Goal: Number of Students	Goal: % of Students
☐	Deficient/Intensive (Tier 3)			
▨	Emerging/Strategic (Tier 2)			
■	Established/Benchmark (Tier 1)			

FIGURE 32. Data from fourth-grade fall DIBELS ORF used for goal setting.

MEETING GRADE-LEVEL GOALS

Once the core team identifies the goals for the next benchmark period, team members must discuss strategies and barriers related to reaching these goals. Another tool useful for core team discussion can be found in Form 18. This tool requires teams to record the specific goals for the next benchmark period, identify barriers and concerns that may be evident in meeting the goals, brainstorm solutions to potential barriers, and select the solution that could best resolve barriers and concerns. This simple tool helps team members discuss openly the opportunities and instructional challenges in making sure that goals are met.

DATA DISPLAYS FOR GRADE-LEVEL MEETINGS

Core team members prepare the data set for examination and interpretation by the grade-level teams. Use of spreadsheets or other forms of data management is essential for efficient discussion at these meetings. Typically, these meetings last from 30 to 45 minutes, during which all students in an entire grade must be discussed. To facilitate the process, data displays need to be simple, easy to understand, and allow quick determination of the impact of the instructional program in place. Although the core team will have carefully examined these data in some detail and made recommendations for student assignment to tiers as well as instructional programs matched to skill needs within those tiers, it is essential that grade-level teams, comprised primarily of instructional staff, have an equal level of skill in interpreting these data.

Each RTI implementation has a particular data display process that works best for it. The data shown in Figure 33 are a portion of reading data from a winter grade-level team meeting for third-grade students. Microsoft Excel was used as the database, and these data were displayed for staff during the meeting. Presented on the spreadsheet were all the relevant data sources, including scores on students' DIBELS oral reading fluency (both WCPM and percentage of accuracy are displayed), the instructional recommendation made by the DIBELS program, scores on a reading maze measure, scores on a group-administered measure of reading comprehension called 4sight benchmark assessment, and the current attained ROI from progress monitoring data for those students at Tier 2 or 3. Both fall and winter scores are displayed along with the core team recommendations. Finally, the data are color coded (shown in shades of gray here) to easily see when a student's score is below benchmark (light gray) or in the at-risk range (dark gray). The data are also divided into those students who were assigned to benchmark, strategic (Tier 2), or intensive (Tier 3) groups based on their fall assessment data. Also indicated on the data display is the specific instructional group to which the student is assigned. In this particular RTI implementation, students at Tier 2 received PALS (Peer Assisted Learning Strategies; *kc.vanderbilt.edu/pals*) at two levels with targets for different reading skills, and students at Tier 3 received different levels of the program SRA Corrective Reading.

Looking down the last column of Figure 33, one can see that the team decisions included changing instructional levels within tiers (Vo was moved to low-benchmark group; C in strategic has an emphasis on comprehension), as well as moving students between tiers (J in strategic was moved to benchmark, given his improvement in scores).

TOOLS FOR INDIVIDUAL STUDENT DECISIONS

At both core and grade-level team meetings, the progress monitoring of those students currently in tiered interventions is examined. Teams need to quickly determine if the data support increasing a student's goal, continuing the student in the current level and type of support, or making an instructional change. In order to facilitate this process, Form 19 can be a useful tool. Each student's name and cur-

| | | | Fall 07 | | | | | | | Winter 08 | | | | | |
Last	First	Teacher	ORF (77)	ORF Acc. > 95%	IR	MAZE (12)	4Sight Prof ≥ 70% Basic = 54–69%	Group	PM ROI	ORF (92)	ORF Acc. > 95%	IR	Maze (13)	4Sight Prof ≥ 70% Basic = 54–69%	Decision
Students in benchmark in fall															
S	M	Z	149	98.7	B	23	77%	B	NA	171	99.4	B	28	90%	Stay
E	V	Z	148	99.3	B	22	83%	B	NA	164	99.4	B	20	80%	Stay
Se	J	W	142	98.6	B	21	77%	B	NA	154	100	B	21	90%	Stay
C	A	Z	140	100	B	19	80%	B (gr4)	NA	142	98.6	B	20	83%	Stay
K	T	Z	134	100	B	20	63%	B	NA	133	99.3	B	26	77%	Stay
L	J	L	127	98.4	B	21	70%	B	NA	119	98.3	B	8	70%	Stay
Vo	K	L	112	97.3	B			B	NA	117	98.1	B	12	50%	Move to low benchmark?
Pi	J	W	108		B	12	63%	B	NA	128	100	B	19	87%	Stay
Po	D	W	106	98.1	B	21	73%	B	NA	145	100	B	23	83%	Stay
G	B	L	92	98.9	B	15	63%	B	NA	87	98.9	S	15	60%	Move to low benchmark?
D	A	W	66	97.1	S	13	80%	B	1.5	91	98.9	S	15	70%	Move to strategic?
Students in strategic in fall															
C	T	L	88	88	B	14	73%	S-PALS	0.2	83	95.4	S	15	67%	Comprehension needs
J	F	L	72	96	S	13	73%	S-PALS	−0	87	97.8	S	15	83%	Stay
P	G	W	72	98.6	S	9	63%	S-PALS	2.2	75	96.2	S	14	67%	Comprehension needs
J	B	W	62	96.9	S	6	57%	S-PALS	2.1	99	98	B	13	70%	Move to benchmark
S	C	Z	58	78.4	S	16	43%	S-PALS	−1	65	95.6	I	14	43%	Stay—fluency needs
F	C	Z	23	100	I	4	23%	S-PALS	0.3	55	98.2	I	6	40%	Stay—slow but accurate reader
Students in intensive in fall															
T	W	L	51	94.4	I	10	43%	I-CR B1	0.7	56	94.9	I	10	70%	Stay
To	F	Z	47	95.9	I	6	27%	I-CR A	2.3	66	91.7	I	12	70%	Move CR B1
He	J	W	45		I		0%	I-CR B1	0	54	90	I	5	50%	Move down to CR A
G	C	L	35	87.5	I	5	43%	I-CR A	0.3	33	89.2	I	5	17%	Stay
Average			79.2	94.7		13.0	0.6		0.9	93.7	95.9		13.4	70%	

% Prof = 67%

FIGURE 33. Example of spreadsheet at a grade-level team meeting of third-grade staff. IR, instructional recommendation; PM ROI, progress monitoring rate of improvement; B, benchmark; S, strategic; I, iIntensive; PALS, Peer Assisted Learning Strategies; CR, corrective reading.

rent instructional level are recorded, and teams examining the progress monitoring data make a determination, including justification for their decision.

EXERCISE IN DATA-BASED DECISION MAKING

Figure 34 presents an opportunity to practice data-based decision making. Data are presented following the fourth-grade winter benchmarking period of a hypothetical classroom. The available data sources for students who were at benchmark at the fall of the school year are the outcomes of the fall and winter D-ORF scores, an indication of whether students achieved the DIBELS benchmark (105 WCPM) for winter, the accuracy of students' performance on the D-ORF (95% or better is expected), and students' percentage correct on the 4sight benchmark assessments (a group-administered measure of reading vocabulary and comprehension) taken at baseline (beginning of school year) and midyear. A score of 57% on this measure represents proficiency. For students assigned to strategic or intensive groups, an indication of the degree to which they achieved the benchmark score of 105 WCPM, as well as whether they achieved the score marking the strategic level (between 83 and 104 WCPM), were noted. In addition, data from students' progress monitoring are provided. The target ROI for each student is provided—that is, the ROI needed for the student to reach the established benchmark goal along with the student's attained ROI throughout the period in which he/she received tiered intervention. Note that the expected or typical ROI for students, based on fall-to-winter benchmarks for the time period, was 0.7 WCPM/week.

Readers are asked to examine those students with gray boxes and to write your decision as to whether each should remain within the tier where he/she is currently assigned, whether his/her goals should be increased, or whether a change should be made. To assist readers further, Figures 35 and 36 provide the actual progress monitoring for each student. An answer key is provided in Figures 37 and 38, where a fuller explanation of the rationale behind the decisions is offered.

Students at Benchmark at Fall of Year

	Fall DORF Score	Winter DORF Score	Reached Winter Bnchmk Target of 105*	Reached Winter Strtgc Target of 83	Winter DORF Accuracy (95%)	4Sight Test 1; 57% = P Total	4Sight Test 3; 57% = P Total	Progress Monitoring Targeted ROI	Progress Monitoring Attained ROI	Decision
Locke, John	128	134	✓		96%	77%	80%			
Shephard, Jack	102	118	✓		95%	53%	57%			
Kwon, Jin-Soo	142	147	✓		97%	70%	73%			
Austen, Kate	103	148	✓		98%	70%	80%			
Reyes, Hugo	133	142	✓		99%	53%	70%			
Littlejohn, Claire	113	140			100%	40%	50%			
Jarrah, Sayid	93	99			96%	42%	44%			

Students at Strategic at Fall of Year

	Fall DORF Score	Winter DORF Score	Reached Winter Bnchmk Target of 105*	Reached Winter Strtgc Target of 83	Winter DORF Accuracy (95%)	4Sight Test 1; 57% = P Total	4Sight Test 3; 57% = P Total	Progress Monitoring Targeted ROI 0.7 = Exp ROI	Progress Monitoring Attained ROI	Decision
Flowers, May	92	106	✓		96%	60%	63%	1.64	2.28	
Showers, April	83	110	✓		94%	73%	67%	1.14	1.56	
Wanka, Willy	75	91		▲	94%	43%	53%	1.14	2.88	
Sam Spade	67	99		▲	93%	43%	67%	1.00	2.01	
Flinstone, Wilma	71	91		▲	98%	67%	70%	1.78	1.85	
Rubble, Barney	73	90			93%	60%	47%	1.00	2.47	

Students at Intensive at Fall of Year

	Fall DORF Score	Winter DORF Score	Reached Winter Bnchmk Target of 105*	Reached Winter Strtgc Target of 83	Winter DORF Accuracy (95%)	4Sight Test 1; 57% = P Total	4Sight Test 3; 57% = P Total	Progress Monitoring Targeted ROI 0.7 = Exp ROI	Progress Monitoring Attained ROI	Decision
Rubble, Betty	51	62			98%	10%	23%	2.47	1.53	
Bush, Rose	43	58			95%	37%	57%	3.60	-0.15	
Lincoln, Abraham	41	60			92%	33%	37%	0.82	1.64	
Bugg, June	49	56			89%	47%	37%	2.20	1.32	
March, Ides	56	92		▲	97%	73%	80%	1.08	4.14	

FIGURE 34. Data for practice in data-based decision making.

176

May Lynn Flowers

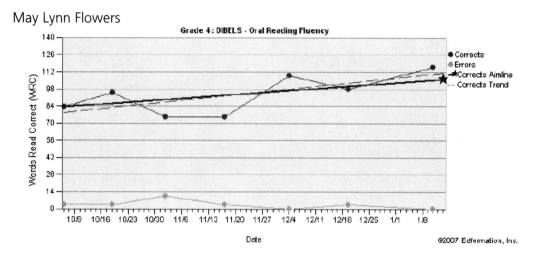

April Lynn Showers

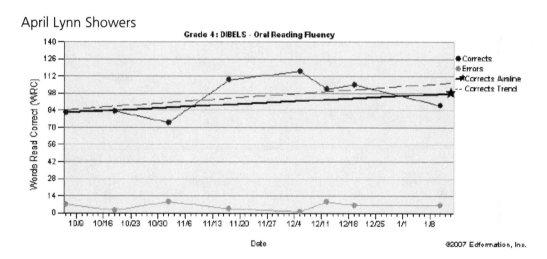

Sam Spade

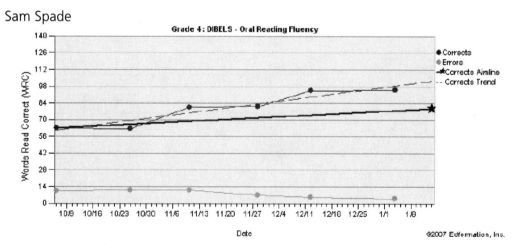

FIGURE 35. Progress monitoring graphs for three fourth-grade students at strategic level in the fall of the year.

Abraham Lincoln

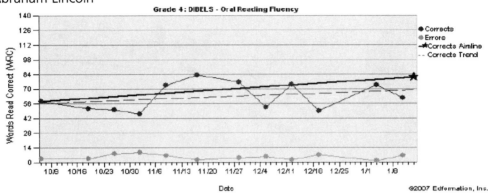

June Bugg

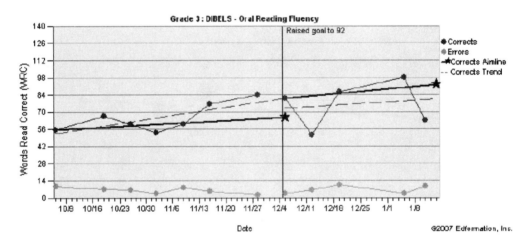

March Ides

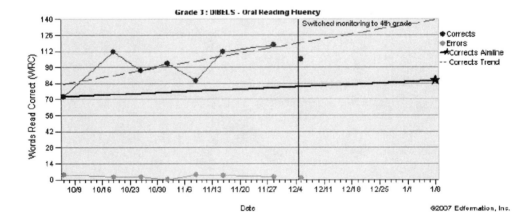

FIGURE 36. Progress monitoring graphs for three fourth-grade students at intensive level in the fall of the year.

Students at Benchmark at Fall of Year

Name	Fall DORF Score	Winter DORF Score	Reached Winter Bnchmk Target of 105*	Reached Winter Strtgc Target of 83	Winter DORF Accuracy (95%)	4Sight Test 1; 57% = P Total	4Sight Test 3; 57% = P Total	Progress Monitoring Targeted ROI	Progress Monitoring Attained ROI	Decision
Locke, John	128	134	✓		96%	77%	80%			
Shephard, Jack	102	118	✓		95%	53%	57%			Continue—on watch—4sight
Kwon, Jin-Soo	142	147	✓		97%	70%	73%			
Austen, Kate	103	148	✓		98%	70%	80%			
Reyes, Hugo	133	142			99%	53%	70%			Continue
Littlejohn, Claire	113	140			100%	40%	50%			
Jarrah, Sayid	93	99			96%	42%	44%			Tier 2 vocab & comp—4sight

Students at Strategic at Fall of Year

Name	Fall DORF Score	Winter DORF Score	Reached Winter Bnchmk Target of 105*	Reached Winter Strtgc Target of 83	Winter DORF Accuracy (95%)	4Sight Test 1; 57% = P Total	4Sight Test 3; 57% = P Total	Progress Monitoring Targeted ROI 0.7 = Exp ROI	Progress Monitoring Attained ROI	Decision
Flowers, May	92	106	✓		96%	60%	63%	1.64	2.28	Exit to Tier 1—PM & 4sight
Showers, April	83	110	✓		94%	73%	67%	1.14	1.56	Exit to Tier 1—PM & 4sight
Wanka, Willy	75	91		◄	94%	43%	53%	1.14	2.88	
Sam Spade	67	99		◄	93%	43%	67%	1.00	2.01	Continue - raise goal
Flinstone, Wilma	71	91		◄	98%	67%	70%	1.78	1.85	
Rubble, Barney	73	90		◄	93%	60%	47%	1.00	2.47	

Students at Intensive at Fall of Year

Name	Fall DORF Score	Winter DORF Score	Reached Winter Bnchmk Target of 105*	Reached Winter Strtgc Target of 83	Winter DORF Accuracy (95%)	4Sight Test 1; 57% = P Total	4Sight Test 3; 57% = P Total	Progress Monitoring Targeted ROI 0.7 = Exp ROI	Progress Monitoring Attained ROI	Decision
Rubble, Betty	51	62			98%	10%	23%	2.47	1.53	
Bush, Rose	43	58			95%	37%	57%	3.60	-0.15	
Lincoln, Abraham	41	60			92%	33%	37%	0.82	1.64	Continue—change in instructional program—comp and fluency
Bugg, June	49	56			89%	47%	37%	2.20	1.32	Continue—change in instructional program—comp and fluency
March, Ides	56	92		◄	97%	73%	80%	1.08	4.14	Exit to Tier 2: Increase in ORF, PM, 4sight

FIGURE 37. Answer key for practice in data-based decision making.

179

Student	Current Tier	Decision	Rationale
Shephard, Jack	1	Continue—on watch—4sight	Well above benchmark in ORF; accuracy is acceptable; 4sight is barely proficient, suggesting some potential struggles in comprehension; on watch with emphasis on comprehension strategies
Reyes, Hugo	1	Continue	Well above benchmark in ORF; highly accurate; 4sight is well above proficient level
Jarrah, Sayid	1	Tier 2	Below ORF benchmark; small gain from fall to winter in ORF; reads accurately, but 4sight is below proficient. Place into instructional group focused on vocabulary building and comprehension
Flowers, May	2	Exit to Tier 1	Reached winter ORF benchmark, maintained accuracy, attained ROI > target ROI; PM graph supports consistent performance; achieved proficiency on 4sight
Showers, April	2	Exit to Tier 1	Reached winter ORF benchmark; accuracy just slightly below expectation; attained ROI > targeted ROI; graph suggests trend that is at or above goal, although slight decline noted on last data point; 4sight remain at proficient
Spade, Sam	2	Continue—raise goal	Did not reach winter ORF benchmark; large increase from fall to winter ORF; accuracy < 95%; attained ROI > target ROI; PM above target.
Lincoln, Abraham	3	Continue—change in instructional program—comp and fluency	Did not reach strategic winter ORF benchmark; accuracy < 95%, attained ROI < target ROI, but attained ROI > expected ROI; 4sight very much below proficient. Emphasis in instructional program needs to shift to work specifically in fluency building and comprehension
Bugg, June	3	Continue—change in instructional program—comp and fluency	Did not reach strategic winter ORF; very small gain fall to winter in ORF; accuracy substantially < 95%; PM had been below grade level; attained ROI < target ROI after goal was raised to 92; 4sight very much below proficient. Emphasis in instructional program needs to shift to work specifically in fluency building and comprehension
March, Ides	3	Exit to Tier 2	Reached strategic winter ORF benchmark; accuracy > 95%; attained ROI > targeted ROI; PM shows ability to succeed at fourth-grade level; 4sight is proficient

FIGURE 38. Rationale for decisions related to tier assignment by team.

LEVEL OF IMPLEMENTATION SCALE—CORE DATA TEAM

Data Analysis	Not Relevant	Not Evident (0 pt)	Partially Evident (1 pt)	Fully Evident (2 pt)
1. Student data are prepared for the meeting in a teacher-friendly format and sent to teachers in advance. The principal decides who is to be the session facilitator and arranges the meeting logistics. *Facilitator:*				
2. Attendees include principal, all data team members, as well as others. *Designated attendees:*				
3. Data team sets measurable goals for each grade level, presented in terms of specific percentages of students reaching proficiency on screening assessments (a specific number is stated for each goal, e.g., *"Right now we have 70% of our first graders at benchmark on the DIBELS Phoneme Segmentation Fluency subtest. By January, 80% of first-grade students will be proficient."*) *Specific goals:*				
4. Data team identifies barriers to meeting goals by designated time and addresses all concerns.				
5. Data team brainstorms ideas to address concerns. Strategies are discussed and those that are most beneficial/feasible to implement are identified.				
6. Data team plans the logistics of implementing agreed-upon strategies in all classrooms in that grade level (at least one specific strategy is discussed for scheduling, intervention implementation, and/or sharing progress monitoring data). *Strategy discussed:*				
7. Data team schedules a time to review the progress of students in follow-up meetings to determine the efficacy of implemented strategies (a specific time and date are set for the follow-up meeting). *Follow-up meeting date/time:*				
8. Data team discusses how to monitor the fidelity of the intervention (at least one strategy is discussed). *Strategy discussed:*				
9. Data team monitors the student's progress.				
10. Data team fine-tunes the strategies.				
TOTAL = _____ / _____ : _____ % Implementation				

LEVEL OF IMPLEMENTATION SCALE—GRADE-LEVEL DATA TEAM

Data Analysis	Not Relevant	Not Evident (0 pt)	Partially Evident (1 pt)	Fully Evident (2 pt)
1. Student data are prepared for the meeting by the classroom teacher and brought to the meeting. A DDMT member acts as facilitator of meeting. *Facilitator:*				
2. Attendees include principal, all teachers from the grade level, and data manager(s) as well as others. *Designated attendees:*				
3. Data team reviews measurable goals set by core team for each grade level, presented in terms of specific percentages of students reaching proficiency on screening assessments (a specific number is stated for each goal, e.g., *"Right now we have 70% of our first graders at benchmark on the DIBELS Phoneme Segmentation Fluency subtest. By January, 80% of first-grade students will be proficient."*) *Specific goals:*				
4. Data team discusses strategies identified by core team to be implemented across all classes.				
5. Grade-level team briefly reviews progress monitoring data to evaluate performance of individual students in terms of which students are above, below, or at target. Based on this evaluation, the team decides which students are in need of instructional or goal changes.				
6. Grade-level team reviews performance of those students identified as in need of a goal or instructional change to determine appropriate action. Decisions regarding changes should be made as a group.				
7. Grade-level teams identify students in need of more support at Tier 2 or Tier 3. *The grade-level teams identify students that will need more frequent assessment. These students include the most deficient students and "stalled" students.*				
8. Grade-level teams discuss how to monitor the fidelity of the intervention (at least one strategy is discussed). *Strategy discussed:*				
9. Grade-level teams fine-tune any strategies being used for Tier 2 and Tier 3 interventions.				
10. Grade-level teams schedule a time to review the progress of students in follow-up meetings to determine the efficacy of implemented changes (a specific time and date are set for the follow-up meeting). *Follow-up meeting date/time:*				
TOTAL = _____ / _____ : _____ % Implementation				

INSTRUCTIONS FOR GOAL-SETTING WORKSHEET:
STRATEGIC TO BENCHMARK

1. Determine the **typical rate of improvement** (**ROI**; look at the AIMSweb or DIBELS Benchmark sheet).

2. Determine **target ROI** (multiply the typical ROI by 1.5).

3. Determine **expected gain** (**EG**).
   a. Multiply the target ROI (your result from Step 2) by the number of weeks till the next benchmark assessment (typically this is an 18-week period).
   b. This is the number of words you expect the students to gain in the coming benchmark period.

4. Calculate the **cutoff score**.
   a. Find the benchmark target for the next assessment period.
   b. Subtract your number from Step 3 from the next benchmark target.
   c. This gives you the cutoff score.

5. **Determine how many students you can expect to get to benchmark**. Determine how many students at the strategic level are at or above the cutoff number (the number you determined in Step 4).
   a. Look at the distribution scores.
   b. Find the cutoff score in the distribution.
   c. Count how many students are at or above that cutoff score. (Remember to count the number of students who are already at benchmark as well.)

6. Convert the number of students you expect to reach or stay at benchmark in time for the next assessment into a **percentage**:
   a. Divide the number of students from Step 5 by the total number of students at the grade level and multiply by 100.
   b. This is the percentage of students you expect to reach benchmark in the next assessment . . . your goal!

GOAL-SETTING WORKSHEET: STRATEGIC TO BENCHMARK

1. Determine the typical rate of improvement (ROI; look at the AIMSweb or DIBELS benchmark sheet).

Typical Rate of Improvement:

2. Determine target ROI (multiply the typical ROI by 1.5).

_____ (Typical ROI) × **1.5** (Multiplier) = _____ (Target ROI)

_____ × _____ = _____

3. Determine expected gain (EG).
   a. Multiply the target ROI (your result from Step 2) by the number of weeks till the next benchmark assessment (typically this is an 18-week period).
   b. This is the number of words you expect the students to gain in the coming benchmark period.

_____ (Typical ROI) × _____ (Number of weeks) = _____ (EG)

_____ × _____ = _____

4. Calculate the cutoff score.
   a. Find the benchmark target for the next assessment period.
   b. Subtract your number from Step 3 from the next benchmark target.
   c. This gives you the cutoff score.

_____ (Next benchmark target) – _____ (EG) = _____ (Cutoff score)

_____ – _____ = _____

(cont.)

5. Determine how many students you can expect to get to benchmark. Determine how many students at the strategic level are at or above the cutoff number (the number you determined in Step 4).
   a. Look at the distribution.
   b. Find the cutoff score in the graph.
   c. Count how many students are at or above that cutoff score. (Remember to count the number of students who are already at benchmark as well.)

Strategic students at or above cutoff number: _____

Number of students already at benchmark: _____

Total number of students expected to be at benchmark by next assessment: _____

6. Convert the number of students you expect to reach or stay at benchmark in time for the next assessment into a percentage:
   a. Divide the number of students from Step 5 by the total number of students at the grade level and multiply by 100.
   b. This is the percentage of students you expect to reach benchmark in the next assessment . . . your goal!

_____ (Total: Step 5) ÷ _____ (Total # of students) = _____ × 100 = _____ %

_____ ÷ _____ = _____ × 100 = _____ %

Goal for next assessment: _____ %

GRADE-LEVEL GOAL REVIEW, BARRIERS, AND SOLUTIONS

1. **Goals:** Goals for the next benchmark period, as determined by the data decision team (using typical rates of improvement multiplied by approximately 1.5)

Grade 2   **Measure: ORF**

Circle Current: Fall or Spring	Current Status		Next Benchmark Goal	
	Number of Students	%	Number of Students	%
Deficient/Intensive (Tier 3)				
Emerging/Strategic (Tier 2)				
Established/Benchmark (Tier 1)				

2. **Barriers and Concerns:** What barriers do you foresee in attaining these goals? What concerns do you have?

3. **Brainstorm:** Brainstorm strategies, supports, materials, training, or services needed to achieve goal(s) for 5–10 minutes. List all suggestions below.

4. Analyze each suggestion above. Consider those that are evidence-based, practical, and feasible within the given time frame. Circle those that meet these criteria.

GRADE-LEVEL MEETING PROGRESS MONITORING DATA-BASED DECISION FORM

Student	Tier	Progress	Decision	Comment
	□ Strategic □ Intensive	□ Above Target □ Near Target □ Below Target	□ Continue □ Raise Goal □ Instructional □ Change/Modification	
	□ Strategic □ Intensive	□ Above Target □ Near Target □ Below Target	□ Continue □ Raise Goal □ Instructional □ Change/Modification	
	□ Strategic □ Intensive	□ Above Target □ Near Target □ Below Target	□ Continue □ Raise Goal □ Instructional □ Change/Modification	
	□ Strategic □ Intensive	□ Above Target □ Near Target □ Below Target	□ Continue □ Raise Goal □ Instructional □ Change/Modification	
	□ Strategic □ Intensive	□ Above Target □ Near Target □ Below Target	□ Continue □ Raise Goal □ Instructional □ Change/Modification	
	□ Strategic □ Intensive	□ Above Target □ Near Target □ Below Target	□ Continue □ Raise Goal □ Instructional □ Change/Modification	
	□ Strategic □ Intensive	□ Above Target □ Near Target □ Below Target	□ Continue □ Raise Goal □ Instructional □ Change/Modification	
	□ Strategic □ Intensive	□ Above Target □ Near Target □ Below Target	□ Continue □ Raise Goal □ Instructional □ Change/Modification	
	□ Strategic □ Intensive	□ Above Target □ Near Target □ Below Target	□ Continue □ Raise Goal □ Instructional □ Change/Modification	
	□ Strategic □ Intensive	□ Above Target □ Near Target □ Below Target	□ Continue □ Raise Goal □ Instructional □ Change/Modification	
	□ Strategic □ Intensive	□ Above Target □ Near Target □ Below Target	□ Continue □ Raise Goal □ Instructional □ Change/Modification	
	□ Strategic □ Intensive	□ Above Target □ Near Target □ Below Target	□ Continue □ Raise Goal □ Instructional □ Change/Modification	

References

Brown-Chidsey, R., Bronaugh, L., & McGraw, K. (2009). *RTI in the classroom: Guidelines and recipes for success*. New York: Guilford Press.

Brown-Chidsey, R., & Steege, M. W. (2010). *Response to intervention: Principles and strategies for effective practice* (2nd ed.). New York: Guilford Press.

Burns, M. K. (2001). Measuring sight-word acquisition and retention rates with curriculum-based assessment. *Journal of Psychoeducational Assessment, 19,* 148–157.

Burns, M. K., & Boice, H. (2009). Comparison of the relationship between words retained and intelligence for three instructional strategies among students with below-average IQ. *School Psychology Review, 38,* 284–292.

DuPaul, G. J., Rapport, M. D., & Perriello, L. M. (1991). Teacher ratings of academic skills: The development of the Academic Performance Rating Scale. *School Psychology Review, 20,* 284–300.

Erion, J., Davenport, C., Rodax, N., Scholl, B., & Hardy, J. (2009). Cover–copy–compare and spelling: One versus three repetitions. *Journal of Behavioral Education, 18,* 319–330.

Fuchs, L. S. (2003). Assessing intervention responsiveness: Conceptual and technical issues. *Learning Disabilities Research and Practice, 18,* 172–186.

Fuchs, L. S., Fuchs, D., Hamlett, C. L., & Allinder, R. M. (1991). Effects of expert system advice within curriculum-based measurement on teacher planning and student achievement in spelling. *School Psychology Review, 20,* 49–66.

Fuchs, L. S., Hamlett, C. L., & Fuchs, D. (1999). *Monitoring basic skills progress: Basic math concepts and applications—blackline masters*. Austin, TX: Pro-Ed.

Gickling, E. E., & Havertape, S. (1981). *Curriculum-based assessment (CBA)*. Minneapolis: School Psychology Inservice Training Network.

Gresham, F. M. (2002). Responsiveness to intervention: An alternative approach to the identification of learning disabilities. In R. Bradley, L. Danielson, & D. P. Hallahan (Eds.), *Identification of learning disabilities: Research to practice* (pp. 467–519). Mahwah, NJ: Erlbaum.

Hargis, C. H., Terhaar-Yonker, M., Williams, P. C., & Reed, M. T. (1988). Repetition requirements for word recognition. *Journal of Reading, 31,* 320–327.

Hasbrouck, J., & Tindal, G. A. (2006). Oral reading fluency: 90 years of measurement. *The Reading Teacher, 59,* 636–644.

MacQuarrie, L. L., Tucker, J. A., Burns, M. L., & Hartman, B. (2002). Comparison of retention rates using traditional, drill sandwich, and incremental rehearsal flash card methods. *School Psychology Review, 31*, 584–595.

Marston, D., Muyskens, P., Lau, M. Y., & Canter, A. (2003). Problem-solving model for decision making with high-incidence disabilities: The Minneapolis experience. *Learning Disabilities Research and Practice, 18*, 187–200.

National Association of State Directors of Special Education (2006). *Response to intervention: Policy considerations and implementation*. Washington, DC: Author.

Rathvon, N. (2008). *Effective school interventions: Strategies for enhancing academic achievement and social competence* (2nd ed). New York: Guilford Press.

Shapiro, E. S. (1990). An integrated model for curriculum-based assessment. *School Psychology Review, 19*, 331–349.

Shapiro, E. S. (2004). *Academic skills problems: Direct assessment and intervention* (3rd ed.). New York: Guilford Press.

Shapiro, E. S. (2011). *Academic skills fourth edition workbook*. New York: Guilford Press.

Shapiro, E. S., Hilt-Panahon, A., & Gischlar, K. L. (in press). Implementing proven research in school-based practices: Progress monitoring within a response-to-intervention model. In M. R. Shinn & H. M. Walker (Eds.), *Interventions for achievement and behavior problems in a three-tier model including RTI*. Washington, DC: National Association of School Psychologists.

Shapiro, E. S., Zigmond, N., Wallace, T., & Marston, D. (Eds.). (in press). *Models of response-to-intervention implementation: Tools, outcomes, and implications*. New York: Guilford Press.

Shinn, M. R. (1988). Development of curriculum-based local norms for use in special education decision-making. *School Psychology Review, 17*, 61–80.

Shinn, M. R. (1989). *Curriculum-based measurement: Assessing special children*. New York: Guilford Press.

Shinn, M. R., & Walker, H. M. (Eds.). (2010). *Interventions for achievement and behavior problems in a three-tier model including RTI*. Washington, DC: National Association of School Psychologists.

Skinner, C. H., Belifore, P. J., & Pearce, N. (1992). Cover, copy, and compare: Increasing georgraphy accuracy in students with behavior disorders. *School Psychology Review, 21*, 73–81.

Skinner, C. H., Turco, T. L., Beatty, K. L., & Rasavage, C. (1989). Cover, copy, and compare: A method for increasing multiplication performance. *School Psychology Review, 18*, 412–420.

Smith, T. J., Ditmer, K. I., & Skinner, C. H. (2002). Enhancing science performance in students with learning disabilities using cover, copy, compare: A student shows the way. *Psychology in the Schools, 39*, 417–426.

Vaughn, S., Linan-Thompson, S., & Hickman, P. (2003). Response to instruction as a means of identifying students with reading/learning disabilities. *Exceptional Children, 69*, 391–409.

Vaughn, S., Wanzek, J., Woodruff, A. L., & Linan-Thompson, S. (2007). Prevention and early identification of students with reading disabilities. In D. Haager, J. Klingner, & S. Vaughn (Eds.), *Evidence-based reading practices for response to intervention* (pp. 11–27). Baltimore: Brookes.

White, O. R., & Haring, N. G. (1980). *Exceptional teaching* (2nd ed.). Columbus, OH: Merrill.